Steady Faith

NAVIGATE THE DETOURS, LIVE YOUR
PURPOSE, MAKE A DIFFERENCE

Dr. Karla P. Scott

IDDO Publishing
Annapolis, Maryland

For Collin and Marye whose loud cheers of encouragement ring out from among that great cloud of witnesses.

CONTENTS

PRAISE FOR *STEADY FAITH*

As I began to read I was completely enthralled by your transparency, confidence in God and determination through fear. Often times we hesitate to move out into deep waters or foreign territory because of fear of the unknown. You remind us that our steps are ordered by God and can't be changed. The purpose that He has placed in us must be fulfilled in accordance to His will and *not* how we feel, or our lack of belief that we are adequate for His purpose. This book is a must read for all believers.

Christine Psalms, Founder and CEO
Dancing for His Glory Studio and Company

Faith is at its finest during life's unexpected turns. My thoughts were immediately captured by the intrigue and universal connectivity in the first chapter. Suspenseful yet beautifully written, it reveals how one moment in time can reveal the purpose for one's life journey!

Mary Perara, President and CEO at 365iNfusion, LLC
and Author of *Priority One*

Steady Faith by Dr. Karla Scott is an exploration of what it truly means to walk by faith and not by sight. Through adventurous, humorous, heartwarming narrative and reflection of God's constant and steady hand at work in her life, each chapter of this book takes us on a remarkable journey all over the world offering a generous glimpse into the life of a woman whose gifts have not only made room for her, but have often placed her in the presence of greatness time after time.

Karla's gems of wisdom gained as a result of her unflinching rock steady solid belief will awaken and inspire the natural born leader in you to walk tall in your purpose and strut by faith, fearless and full of grace.

Stacey Evans Morgan, Television Producer/Writer and author of the novel *A Good Thing*

If you serve in any capacity of leadership, let *Steady Faith* be the navigation system that guides you into becoming an Influential Leader. Truly, this book is designed to escort fervent Change Agents through their personal journey to discover or reconnect to their God ordained purpose as a Leader. Ultimately, I am convinced that *Steady Faith* can be one of the major tools which leaders, both secular and sacred, can employ as they endeavor to make an indelible impact in the lives of those they serve.

Mrs. Kelly Gorham, Supervised Therapist & Crisis Responder, VMCL, Certified Coach Practitioner, CCF IWN Internet Radio Host

INTRODUCTION

The year before I wrote this book, I completed a doctoral degree that required a written dissertation. In that project I examined the intersections between gospel music, American nationalism, and military leadership development. The topic is unusual, but I based it on my perspective after serving as the United States Naval Academy Gospel Choir director for a decade. Nationalism and leadership development are fairly academic subjects, but when I presented my research to the faculty committee, they all encouraged me to distribute my findings to the general public.

So I shared my dissertation project with a Christian publicist, who suggested that I combine the academic research and personal story to create an inspirational memoir. She insisted that people would be encouraged if I shared the journey of how I got to the Academy, as well as lessons learned about leadership after ten years in that environment.

To be honest, I had no desire to write something as personal as a memoir, and I didn't think anyone would be interested in stories from my life. I politely said I'd think about it. Unable to forget her suggestion, I began to review years of emails, letters from students, tour schedules, and videos and photos from my work with the choir. Before I knew it, a story of God's faithfulness began to emerge. I found myself connecting the dots, and I realized that for years in advance, the Lord had been preparing me to lead leaders at the Academy and beyond.

In this book you'll read frequent and explicit references to God and the scriptures. This is because I don't know how to tell my story without discussing God, his Word, and my relationship with both. He is the center and the foundation of my life.

My time at the Naval Academy radically changed the way I saw military culture and leadership. Nigerian author Chimamanda Adichie calls stereotypes a "single story."[1] Ten years ago I believed a single story about military officers. I saw them as tough, emotionless, and combat-ready. That assessment was incomplete. Although they many times possess those qualities, their humanity does not magically disappear in the process.

These days I would attribute characteristics such as genuine, unpretentious, and consistent to members of military community. Their service is a demonstration of unwavering love for this nation and its people. I am thankful for the chaplains, counselors, and colleagues who support our military

---

[1] Chimamanda Ngozi Adichie, "The Danger of a Single Story," TED.com. Filmed July 2009 in Oxford, UK. TED video, 18:49. Accessed April 1, 2017.
https://www.ted.com/talks/chimamanda_adichie_the_danger_of_a_single_story.

members, and I am grateful that I had a chance to serve young officers-in-training similarly.

Except for Marine aviator Zerbin Singleton, who gave me permission to use his name and story, I have omitted or changed the names of military officers and former students to avoid bringing attention to those on active duty. I have used the actual names of living civilian colleagues and deceased historical figures.

The book's title is inspired by a phrase in a familiar Academy prayer. It's called "The Midshipman Prayer" and reads in part:

> Almighty God, whose way is in the sea, whose paths are in the great waters, whose command is over all and whose love never faileth; let me be aware of Thy presence and obedient to Thy will.... If I am inclined to doubt, *steady my faith*....[2]

When I read the words "steady my faith" during the writing of this book, they leapt off the page, and I began to recall moments from my life before and during my tenure at the Academy when I needed the Lord to do just that for me. Each time I needed him to anchor me, he did. Shortening the title to *Steady Faith* felt right.

---

[2] "The Midshipman Prayer (Interfaith Version)." United States Naval Academy. Accessed April 1, 2017. https://www.usna.edu/Chapel/nondemprayer.php. (my emphasis added to quotation)

Practical Faith

During my junior year of undergraduate school, I was finally allowed to have a car on campus. I can still remember the thrill of buying that car with my own money and preparing for my first road trip. My university was a three-hour drive from home, and this was long before GPS or Google Maps existed. My dad taught me the basics of navigating the highway system. To this day, when I'm in a new city, I remember that roads ending in zero or even numbers generally run east and west, while those ending in odd numbers typically run north and south. To get to school, I had to head east and navigate four highways. My dad made it sound simple, and turns out, it was. When I arrived on campus safe and sound, I grinned from ear to ear for the rest of the day. Success!

Riding in the Cradle

After making the trip a few times, I developed confidence in my ability to drive long distances, even if I faced unexpected detours. When I had to drive at night, I used another technique called "riding in the cradle," which means to drive sandwiched between two eighteen-wheelers—one in front and one behind. As long as I kept pace with the lead truck, I made excellent time and never felt like I was making the long journey alone. If I began to slow down too much or got distracted, the rear truck would alert me, as its bright high beams flooded my car with light. This was a good reminder to stay focused and on pace. Often as I would turn off that particular stretch of highway to pick up the next interstate, the truckers who formed my cradle would give me a farewell blast on their horns. The kindness of strangers never failed to show up on those road trips to and from school.

I believe that the Gospel Choir at the Naval Academy is like "riding in the cradle" for its midshipmen members. It's a secure place between the pull of the lead truck (military leadership development) and the push of the rear truck (anchoring faith). Students use the Gospel Choir to strike a balance between the two.

My prayer while at the Naval Academy was that when they transitioned from midshipmen to commissioned officers, they would be headed in the right direction, spiritually speaking. I gave thought to the impact that our songs, scriptural teaching, prayers, and fellowship would have on young officers when they eventually deployed. It was always my desire to plant good seeds in their hearts and minds, seeds that would benefit, encourage, and strengthen them when they'd need it most.

The Leader in You

While my natural skills and abilities helped me to lead the choir musically, it was the Lord who taught me how to influence midshipmen in matters of character and spiritual development. If I am honest, I never saw that part coming, but I am richer for the experience because of following the Lord's lead.

Are you a leader? Do others follow your example? Do others seek your counsel or advice? Does your life influence others? It may surprise you to know that the answer to all of these questions is "Yes." It doesn't matter if you consider yourself ordinary or special, an unlikely leader or someone who is destined to lead—we all influence others to some degree. As you read this part of my story—one filled with experiences that led to a certain destiny—I hope you'll be encouraged to continue your journey to become a better influencer.

You may carry the title of student, minister, businessperson, teacher, mom, or something else. Whatever life requires of you, please know that the Lord will provide anchors for your journey, just as the truckers did for me and the Gospel Choir does for midshipmen.

Contact me: www.karlascott.net   Enjoy the book!

Terms You Should Know

Brigade of Midshipmen: The entire student body at the US Naval Academy.

Fleet: A country's navy.

Herndon/Herndon Climb: A gray monument across from the Academy chapel that resembles the Washington Monument in miniature (only twenty-one feet tall). At the end of plebe year, the entire class builds a human pyramid while attempting to climb to the top of the monument, which has been covered in lard.

Midshipman: Refers to any student enrolled at the Academy. Also called *mid, mids,* or *MIDN.*

Officer Representative: A military member who provides oversight for student clubs, groups, and teams at the Naval Academy. Also called *O-Rep* or *Rep.*

SAT: Satisfactory. It refers to the way a midshipman conducts himself or herself as it relates to conduct, grades, honor, military bearing, and more. Upon graduation and entering the fleet, this term will refer to meeting the specific requirements deemed appropriate.

UNSAT: Unsatisfactory. The failure to meet the requirements mentioned above under *SAT*.

United States Naval Academy: A four-year college and military training school that produces commissioned officers for the US Navy and Marine Corps.

United States Naval Academy Classes:

Plebe—Also known as *4/C* or *freshman*. The term *plebe* gets changed to *fourth class* after the completion of Herndon. At commissioning plebes are referred to as *third class*, indicating the start of their sophomore year.

Youngster—Also known as *3/C*, *third class*, or *sophomore*. The name is conferred once they see the chapel dome after returning to the Academy following summer cruise. Up until that time, they are referred to as *third class*.

Second Class—Also known as *2/C* or *junior*. They are officially upperclassmen, which means they can have cars and wear civilian clothes during liberty.

Firstie(s)—Also known as *1/C*, *first class*, or seniors. They function as junior officers, which means manning leadership positions in student clubs at the company or brigade level, along with other campus leadership positions.

CHAPTER ONE

THE MANDARIN LESSON

THE POWER OF PURPOSE

天堂生下我的能力必須有用
If heaven made him, earth can find some use for him.
—*Chinese Proverb*

It wasn't exactly what I'd expected. I stepped across the threshold of the room that would be my home for the next two weeks. Along one wall sat a single bed, and on the opposite wall stood a plain wooden bookshelf and a metal chair. Under the room's only window sat a well-used wooden desk. Through the open window, I caught a glimpse of an apartment building partially hidden by trees and flowering bushes.

Every so often a warm breeze that smelled like flowers and bus exhaust would fill the room. Stark white paint and a stone floor made the room feel clean but impersonal. Beijing, China, in the spring of 1997 seemed intriguing to me—so far. After a twelve-hour flight the day before, I had arrived safely on campus at the China Conservatory of Music. I told myself the room would be fine, especially since I'd be doing little more than sleeping there for the next fourteen days.

The main reason I had traveled to China was to assist my voice teacher. She'd been invited to serve as Artist in Residence at the conservatory. But I did have another reason for coming to Beijing, one that I didn't even tell my teacher. I wanted to meet Pastor Allen Yuan, a leader in the underground house-church movement in China.[3]

In the 1940s, China's house-church movement began in opposition to the government-sanctioned church. After World War II many house-church leaders like Yuan and Watchman Nee were imprisoned for teaching the uncensored Word of God.

I knew how precious Bibles in Mandarin were to underground Christians, so I purchased and brought a few copies with me. My decision to bring them wasn't exactly a safe course of action, and I am not sure what might have happened to me if they had been discovered—but that didn't stop me from facing a moment of anxiety just as I stepped foot in China.

---

[3] "The Faithful Servant—Allen Yuan Xiangchen." ccfellow.org. Accessed April 6, 2017.
http://www.ccfellow.org/Common/Reader/News/ShowNews.jsp?Nid=7048&Pid=22&Version=40&Cid=226&Charset=big5_hkscs—as taken from: Lydia Lee, *Living Sacrifice: The Life Story of Allen Yuan* (Singapore: Singapore Every Home Crusade, 1999).

Facing Fear

When I arrived at Beijing Capital International Airport and headed toward security, I watched agents tear through the luggage of the man in front of me under the careful observation of an armed guard. I noticed that the guard's hand never left his weapon.

Feeling my heart begin to race, I stood in line and did the only thing I could: I prayed for God's intervention. I hadn't thought to hide the Bibles in my luggage, so they were in the shopping bag I held in my left hand. There was no way they would be missed. When the security agent turned to me, I took a deep breath and placed my things on the table to be searched. He motioned for me to pick up my bags and move toward the exit. It took several seconds for me to realize he was not going to search any of my belongings, but instead simply waved me through the line! Stunned and grateful, I hurried off before he changed his mind. I had just experienced a miracle.

Staring Contest

My first week in Beijing was filled with meeting students, observing music rehearsals and even teaching voice lessons to the students who weren't given a spot in my teacher's classes. After school our tour guide took us sightseeing or to nearby shops and restaurants. I expected the large volume of cars on the roads, but I was surprised by how many people rode bicycles, even on major roadways.

Also, Beijing was so densely populated that I'd thought our little group of Americans would blend in. How wrong I was. We drew crowds everywhere we went. Instead of the anonymity I had experienced in London, Rome, New York, and Los Angeles, imagine my surprise when I saw people fall off their bikes because they couldn't stop staring at the four of us: me, my teacher, and my teacher's daughter and her husband. In 1997 our brown skin caused quite a stir there.

Little kids would sometimes run up to us and poke our legs to see if we were real. When we smiled or laughed at their curiosity, they smiled back, but clearly they were rattled. Apparently, no category existed in their brains to account for people who looked like we did. If we stopped as a group to look at a sign, a large crowd of people would instantly form behind us. We'd turn around to face the people, who would be staring, pointing, or covering their mouths in surprise. It felt wild. Most adults, especially the elderly ones, stared so long that it actually became uncomfortable. Our tour guide explained that people of African descent were an infrequent sight in Beijing, so we did our best to take their reactions in stride. Constantly being on display was challenging, though.

We continued to sightsee, visiting temples, gardens, and palaces, and we even climbed a section of the Great Wall. I enjoyed walking through the market streets lined with herbs in woven baskets, or butcher shops with meat hanging from hooks. We saw bold, colorful signage everywhere, and we breathed in the aroma of delicious food coming from countless restaurants. By the end of the first week, we were used to being in China, but the Chinese were not used to us. I woke up every day feeling like an American who happened to be in China, but before long I felt like a spectacle instead of a fellow human being.

The constant stares and attention were more annoying than hurtful. Having been raised in the southern United States, I'd experienced the sting of racism many times, but at least the stares and reactions I received in Beijing seemed motivated by curiosity, not hatred.

The Ceramic Effect

By the end of my trip it dawned on me that although Chinese people viewed me as a foreigner, their stares and thoughts had no power to change who I was. Later, when I was writing this book, I thought back to my first impressions of ceramic pans with the white cooking surface. When I began using this kind of cookware, I felt sure that the food I was preparing would stain or damage it, but that never happened. Just like any other pot or pan, the food that I cooked went from raw to tenderized, delicious, and fully prepared. After a bit of soap and water, the cooking surface was as white as ever.

Purpose and influence have similar staying power. Since God determines the purpose for each of our lives, no one else can ever destroy it. At best, life circumstances and choices can delay the fulfillment of our purpose, but the Lord has a way of making all detours work to our advantage. Similarly true influencers leave situations better than they find them. Their beliefs, words, and deeds have the power to transform.

Proper influence increases effectiveness.

In retrospect, during my trip to Beijing, the Lord revealed my purpose and trained me to be an influencer. By teaching, delivering Bibles, and showing kindness to folks who didn't quite know what to make of me, God positioned me to display his goodness.

The Frail Giant

At the end of my first week in Beijing, I contacted Pastor Yuan, and he came to the conservatory to meet me in person. As he walked toward me, I was startled by his appearance. I had never seen anyone so thin and frail. Dressed in a tan shirt and pants that seemed far too roomy for his frame, he moved with surprising speed. We sat in the dorm's main lobby and began to talk. I was curious about how he knew where to find me on campus. He told me he had asked for "the foreigner" at the gate. I was taken aback by his response, yet drawn to his directness. His voice was slightly hoarse, but he spoke flawless English that was both precise and economical – he didn't mince words.

I explained how the American ministry where I'd purchased the Bibles had given me his name and contact information. We talked about my deep respect for Watchman Nee's books, and he told me that when Nee had been released from prison, Yuan and his wife had allowed him to stay in their home. I can't remember if I gasped out loud when he said that, but I definitely got goose bumps. It was like someone casually saying, "I let Billy Graham live with me for a few months when he needed a place." The fact that I was sitting inches away from a giant in the faith was beginning to sink in for me.

Then I gave him the Bibles I'd brought. He looked in the shopping bag and asked, "Only these?"

"Yes, only these," I replied weakly.

I guess I should have brought more Bibles, I thought.

Suddenly I didn't feel so confident about the gift I'd brought, but before I could apologize, everything shifted.

He leaned forward in his chair and began telling me his testimony of being jailed for pastoring an underground church. "I have suffered untold hardship, imprisoned for over twenty years. I had no Bible, only a few hymns to sustain my faith...."

For the next half hour he told me the details of his imprisonment, torture, time away from his family, and of the God he had clung to through it all. He spoke without raising his voice, but his demeanor changed. I watched as strength filled his body and deepened his voice. The atmosphere in the room became electric with the presence of God. By the time his testimony ended, I was in tears. Without missing a beat, he looked at me and said, "You will come and preach to us."

His blunt words stopped my tears immediately. I protested, but he insisted. In one quick motion he stood up, wrote directions on a slip of paper in Chinese, and told me to hand it to a taxi driver the next morning, which was Sunday. With that, the frail man with the giant spirit walked out of the dormitory.

Have you ever experienced a moment in life that felt like a scene from a movie? I couldn't believe what had just happened. I'd met one of the heroes of the faith, and he wanted *me* to come and speak at his church? My inner monologue sounded something like this:

This can't be real. I am not a preacher. I don't speak Chinese. A strange taxi driver could take me anywhere. Isn't that exactly how people die in the movies? I'm not the one. I won't do it.

I know, I know, my inner dialogue sounded pretty theatrical. All the while, deep down I knew I would go. I had already brought Bibles into a foreign country, so I figured that I might as well continue the adventure.

Taxis, Trust, and Truth

The next morning I stood at the gate of the conservatory. A few students asked what I was waiting for. When I told them I was waiting for a taxi, they laughed and wished me luck, but said taxis didn't come there on Sundays. While they were still speaking, a cab drove toward us and stopped. I got in, handed the directions to the driver, and spent the next several seconds wondering what I had gotten myself into. I don't remember how long the drive took, but I'll never forget the atmosphere inside that taxi.

The song playing on the radio was sung in Mandarin, so I couldn't understand the words. I have no logical explanation, but the peace of God filled that car. It felt like I was listening to worship music. To this day I don't know if the Lord or Pastor Yuan had arranged that taxi and driver, but the entire thing seemed divinely orchestrated.

The taxi driver stopped mid block in a humble part of town. There I was, a very tall, African American woman dressed in a pale yellow dress. I'm sure I stood out like twelve sore thumbs. A casually dressed man approached me, speaking Mandarin. After a few false starts I realized his connection to Pastor Yuan, and I followed him into a narrow alley that immediately became a combination obstacle course and maze. He trotted along quickly, and I was struggling to keep up when suddenly he stopped at an open door to my left. He led me into a single-room house divided into two sections: kitchen and bedroom.

Unexpected Power

Eleven or twelve steps marked the distance between front door and the back wall of Yuan's home. The tiny space was packed with about fifteen people. Weeping and bent in prayer, the majority were women. When I saw the small drinking glasses clutched in their hands, I realized they were taking communion. The juice in their glasses was so diluted that it looked like pale purple water. In the few seconds it took to assess my surroundings, I felt overwhelmed by something familiar—the presence of God. His presence was so strong that by the time I walked the few short steps from the door to the bed (which served as a pulpit), my face was wet with tears and my soul was on fire.

The believers sang and wept, their voices just above a whisper as Pastor Yuan told the story of the last supper. He began to translate everything he was saying into English once I arrived. We took communion and then prayed. I shared a short message from 2 Corinthians 4 as Yuan translated for the congregation. The message seemed well received, judging by the frequent call of "Amen" that I heard.

After the service I met each member, including two young women intent on becoming missionaries in a remote Chinese province. I wanted to take photos of my new friends, but Pastor Yuan advised me not to. He said that if my camera ended up being confiscated as I left China, it would have meant trouble for the people in the photos. It dawned on me that I had preached the Word of God for the first time in my life and that the Lord had taken me to the other side of the world to deliver the message. I looked around the tiny room and noticed a few photos on the wall. I saw a photo of Billy Graham preaching—in the same room. I saw another picture of David Yonggi Cho (pastor of the largest church in South Korea)—teaching from the same pulpit/bed. I was startled to see such towering Christian figures photographed where I'd sat just moments before.

After the church members left, I ate a simple meal with Pastor Yuan and his wife, during which they shared more details about their lives as believers. Today, twenty years later, I am still humbled by all the Lord did that day, and I hold those moments in my heart like priceless treasures.

During that trip God confirmed my identity and purpose. He led me safely through dangerous and uncomfortable circumstances to show me a glimpse of what he'd called me to do—to serve and influence others for him. It may seem strange to have travelled all the way to China to discover this, but the Bible contains countless stories about the Lord plucking people from obscurity and repositioning them to accomplish tasks for his glory.

Sometimes, God confirms identity and purpose in uncomfortable circumstances.

One of my favorite examples of God confirming his purpose in strange circumstances involves a young man named David. He was the youngest of eight sons, and as a result he was given the most menial job in the household—taking care of sheep.

The Unlikely King

One day the prophet Samuel came to speak to David's father, Jesse. God told Samuel that one of Jesse's sons would be the next king of Israel. It was the prophet's job to determine which son the Lord had chosen, then pour oil on his head and announce God's plan. Samuel arrived, met son after son, but the Lord was silent. Jesse mentioned that he had one more out in the fields tending the sheep; apparently thinking there was no way the Lord would want David. You can probably guess how this ends.

In came David, sheepishly (sorry, couldn't re-sist!). I'll bet they could smell him before they could see him. Immediately God confirmed it: David was the chosen one. The prophet poured oil on David's head and announced that the Lord had chosen him as the next king of Israel (see 1 Samuel 16:1-13 for the full story).

God plucked David from obscurity to establish his identity and purpose. For many of you reading this book, He will do the same. At some point in your life, if it hasn't already happened, the Lord will single you out and point you on the road to your destiny. While others struggle to figure out what's going on with you, God will remain faithful to unfold his plan for your life. He promises in Psalm 139:16, "All the days ordained for me were written in your book before one of them came to be." In other words some things will happen in your life because they are part of God's will for you and no one can stop them.

Before I go any further, let me clarify something. This book is not about China or ceramic pans or shepherds. It is about influence, a word in my opinion that is synonymous with leadership.

Why does that matter to you?

It matters because you are called to influence others whether you realize it or not. Sometimes it's easier to see ourselves in the stories of others, so I offer you parts of mine in this book. The scriptures declare, "As iron sharpens iron, so one person sharpens another" (Prov. 27:17).

"As iron sharpens iron, so one person sharpens another."

Like David, the shepherd who became king, the Lord carefully prepared me for the work I would do at the United States Naval Academy in Annapolis, Maryland. Sometimes that preparation included seasons when I felt overlooked or forgotten – as though my life was a series of detours. That's only part of the story. My season of preparation also included times when my gifts and talents were put on display around the world. For a decade, though, I was privileged to serve and influence young military leaders at the Naval Academy as the Director of the Gospel Choir. I use the word *serve* intentionally because I have learned that service to others is a key to lasting influence.

Service to others is a key to lasting influence.

Not only is this book about what happens when preparation, influence and faith in God collide, but it's also about the second assignment the Lord gave me at the Academy: to encourage unity and ethnic diversity within the Gospel Choir and ultimately among future military leaders. I've seen firsthand how unity and diversity brings strength to teams in ways exclusion and division never could. Now, more than ever, unity must be championed by the church in America as a way to combat the divisiveness running rampant in our nation. Fostering unity is part of our purpose as the body of Christ, so let us seek to stay on mission for God always!

CHAPTER TWO

BLUE & GOLD AND BROWN

THE POWER OF ASSIGNMENT

"I feel it is unfortunate the American people have not matured enough to accept an individual on the basis of his ability and not regard a person as an oddity because of his color."[4]
—Retired LCDR Wesley Brown

From its beginnings in Annapolis, Maryland, on the banks of the Severn River in 1845, to its temporary home in Newport, Rhode Island, during the Civil War, the United States Naval Academy has been a training ground for Navy and

---

[4] Paul Vitello, "Wesley Brown, Pioneer as Black Naval Graduate, Dies at 85," *The New York Times*, May 24, 2012. Accessed April 1, 2017. http://www.nytimes.com/2012/05/25/us/wesley-brown-first-black-naval-graduate-dies-at-85.html.

Marine Corps officers for nearly two centuries. After World War II our nation began to expand its view of what it meant to be an American. In academic circles, this viewpoint is termed, *nationalism*. As a result of the rise of a branch of nationalism called *multi-culturalism*, various ethnic groups and eventually women were allowed to participate in all aspects of society. Military service academies slowly embraced those societal changes, and over a century after its founding, the Naval Academy and midshipman Wesley Brown made history.

In 1949, Brown became the first African American to graduate and become a commissioned naval officer.[5] Although he was not the first African American male to enroll at the Academy, Brown was the first to complete all four years. I had the pleasure of meeting Lieutenant Commander (LCDR) Brown on many occasions before his death in 2012. He and his wife were unfailing supporters of the Naval Academy's Gospel Choir and regularly attended concerts. I was honored to know them. His good humor and persevering spirit were evident even though many decades had passed since his time as a midshipman.

LCDR Brown personally invited the Gospel Choir to perform at the opening of the Wesley Brown Field House, built and dedicated in his honor in 2008. He led the way for African American en-

55 Robert John Schneller, *Blue & Gold and Black: Racial Integration of the U.S. Naval Academy* (College Station, TX: Texas A&M University Press, 2008), 23.

rollment in the late 1940s, and by 1976 the Academy was charting new territory again by opening its doors to admit female midshipmen. Decades later the presence of both ethnic minorities and women have become more commonplace as strides toward inclusion were made within Academy culture.

Academy Culture Changes

Bolstered by minority recruitment efforts of the late 1960s and the 1970s, the Navy slowly began to overcome its perception as the most racist branch of the military.[6] By 1985 a group of twenty-three African American midshipmen—inspired by the two-hundred-voice Cadet Gospel Choir at West Point—decided to form a choir of their own.[7] Dr. Barry Talley, Director of Musical Activities at the Naval Academy from 1971–2006 noted, "All the program additions including Gospel Choir and Women's Glee Club were made in response to midshipmen calls for opportunity…. It became apparent to me that [they] were vitally important in feeding the spirit of the midshipmen."[8] After the choir functioned as a student-led organization for several years, Talley hired a professional director for the

[6] Schneller, *Blue & Gold and Black*, 177.

[7] Karla Scott, *Gospel Music Training, Performance Practice and Its Impact on Leadership Development and Performed Nationalism in a Collegiate Military Choir* (PhD diss. University of Maryland, 2015), 55.

[8] Scott, *Gospel Music Training*, 55.

Gospel Choir in 1989. (I'll talk more about that later.)

A Fresh Start

In August 2006, just two weeks before the fall semester started, I received an email about the Gospel Choir director position from my friend, Dr. Lester Green. I responded to the email, took the interview, and was hired on the spot. I was caught off guard by how quickly the offer had come, but as it turned out, I was the only applicant.

I felt confident in my ability to handle the position, perhaps overly so. Gospel music existed outside the boundaries of my formal training, and I'd heard it much more than I'd sung it before coming to the Academy.

At that point I held both a bachelor's and a master's degree in voice and had performed as a classical singer in the US and Europe. As discussed earlier, I had teaching experience in Asia. My first teaching job as Instructor of Music at Bennett College preceded my service in several churches as worship leader and choir director. I had also worked as an accompanist and workshop clinician. *What more could this new Gospel Choir position require?* I figured.

I would soon discover that teaching gospel music in a military setting required skills that nothing in my musical background had fully prepared me for. Looking back on that time, I am reminded of 2 Corinthians 12:9, where the Lord promised the apostle Paul, "My grace is sufficient for you, for my power is made perfect in weakness." I lived out that scripture during my early days at the Academy. Today I understand that every challenge was designed to get me in step with God's plan for the choir and a new season in my life.

The First Rehearsal

At my first rehearsal in late August 2006, I knew I had walked into an unusual environment. The atmosphere was intense, fast paced, and regimented. The choir comprised about thirty students and was accompanied by a band with three civilian gospel musicians: a keyboard player, guitar player, and drummer. Also present at the rehearsal were the military members who provided leadership oversight: a Marine captain, a Marine gunnery sergeant (GySgt), and an enlisted sailor.

I asked the choir to sing songs from the previous year so that I could watch them perform and hear their sound. As they sang, danced, and clapped like a well-oiled machine, I discerned excellent training, high energy, and a focus on performance instead of worship. As soon as the mini-concert was over, the room erupted into loud talking. The GySgt quickly silenced everyone. When he addressed the choir, the intimidation felt palpable to me. I made a note to myself to run a tightly paced rehearsal to minimize talking. I also decided to call the GySgt if I ever needed a bouncer in my personal life.

Strategy for Success

My initial rehearsal strategy was twofold. First I would begin each rehearsal with a predictable sequence: prayer and warm-ups. To close the rehearsal, I would ask leadership to make announcements, then encourage students to share a praise report or prayer request.

The second part of my strategy was to learn the music that the choir already knew. The previous director had completed a recording with the choir before resigning, and a CD release concert was planned for that October. I had about sixty days to get up to speed. The former director graciously came in and conducted a few rehearsals in September and October. I learned valuable rehearsal pacing tips from watching her.

A Series of Challenges

As expected, the challenges I experienced that first year ran the gamut. Early on it became obvious that my personality and teaching style didn't meet the expectations of the military members assigned to the choir. As an encourager by nature, I'd always run musical rehearsals that were focused but lighthearted. Teaching, learning, and retention took place, but in an atmosphere that encouraged joy and laughter.

Creativity flourishes in environments that balance discipline and joy.

I got the sense that the Gospel Choir wasn't meant to be a creative or spiritual endeavor, primarily. In other words choir members were expected to comport themselves seriously even while singing upbeat, enthusiastic music. In the beginning I tried to impart bits of wisdom from the scripture or offer praise for a job well done. I was repeatedly told to display a more stern and aggressive demeanor, and to withhold encouragement until it had been earned. To be honest, I struggled with the idea of using aggression with the choir. It didn't feel like I was true to myself, nor did an aggressive attitude seem to serve the message of the music.

I also faced the steep learning curve of memorizing military jargon and Naval Academy regulations, a process that seemed never-ending. The military had abbreviations for everything, and at first I had a hard time keeping up. I didn't know the difference between SAT and UNSAT, or what a PRT was. When I heard the term "fried" I thought of food, and when someone said "youngster," I thought of a preschooler.[9]

Musically I came face to face with the distinctions between gospel and classical music, and realized I had much to learn about set lists and rehearsal planning. I needed to manage countless details before every performance or tour, details that often needed to be vetted by levels of hierarchy through seemingly endless email chains. I had never felt more like a civilian in my life.

Learning the ropes was stressful and overwhelming, but the greatest challenge was having to perform gospel music without mentioning God to the choir. I understood that the military and the church were two different entities, but I was not prepared to be silent about God or his Word. My early attempts to ignore ministry and focus only on music took a toll on me and produced incredible anxiety.

It Was All a Mistake

By December 2006, just a few short months after taking the job, I began to doubt that the position was for me. Each time I would drive onto the base, my anxiety levels would build until I felt knots in my stomach. Music-making had always been a joy-

[9] SAT is a military term meaning *satisfactory*, while UNSAT means *unsatisfactory*. These terms are applied to standards relating to academics, honor, and physical fitness. PRT (physical readiness test) is a required fitness test administered several times yearly. "Fried" refers to receiving demerits, and "youngster" is the term given to sophomores at the Academy.

ful experience for me, but I dreaded Naval Academy Gospel Choir rehearsals. When Christmas break began, I decided to finish out the school year and hand in my resignation in May.

As the spring semester began in January 2007, the Holy Spirit prompted me to send out requests for prayer. I knew that I would need prayer—and great quantities of antacid—to continue working in an environment I didn't enjoy. I sent a request to several ministries, and while I'm sure all the ministries prayed, only one wrote a response to me. It turned out to be exactly what I needed.

A Word from God

Here are excerpts from the letter I received:

We have prayed over your prayer request. We appreciate how much you want to serve the Lord in your work and understand your desire to see all come to know Jesus as Lord. You are in a unique place and have the opportunity to impact lives that may one day be presidents, vice presidents, members of Congress, judges, lawyers, doctors, generals, and colonels, and so forth. What an awesome assignment.

This is going to be a learning process for you that will continue for years to come. Plant seeds as the Lord directs, and seek the Lord's direction regarding every song and every concert.

Some are called to plant, some to water, and some to harvest. It may be years before you look back and realize all God has done in you and through you in this assignment.

As I re-read that letter now a decade later, I see how prophetic its message was. To be honest, the situation did not improve right away, but by the end of that first school year, I was sure the Lord had planted me at the Academy to complete an assignment. In the words of Ravi Zacharias, "There is no greater discovery than seeing God as the author of your destiny."[10]

"There is no greater discovery than seeing God as the author of your destiny."

This assurance gave me courage as I continued to learn the ropes. I had a strong desire to see my students come to know Christ, but instead of forcing the issue, I trusted the Lord to give me the right strategies for the midshipmen. After all, he knew them intimately. Although it would be many years before I drove onto the Naval Academy base without feeling anxious, I wanted to do God's will, and that inspired me to continue. God used the wisdom in that letter to broaden my perspective. What I learned is this: your assignments in life have more to do with God's will than your comfort.

[10]Ravi K. Zacharias with R. S. B. Sawyer, *Walking from East to West: God in the Shadows* (Grand Rapids, MI: Zondervan, 2010), 240.

When in Doubt, Run!

The desire to disconnect and flee from uncomfortable situations is profoundly human. Jonah ran from his assignment at Nineveh. King Saul ran ahead of the will of God by refusing to wait for the prophet Samuel's sacrifice. David ran from King Saul to King Achish while doing his best impression of a lunatic. Even the mighty prophet Elijah ran from Jezebel's threats just days after defeating her false prophets. When we run from uncomfortable situations, we risk missing the very experiences that prepare us for the future. I know that facing challenges is easier said than done, but it may help to think of challenges as keys in disguise.

Challenges are often keys in disguise.

In the natural world keys are used to unlock doors, vehicles, storage units, and much more. Keys do the same thing in the spiritual realm: they open doors of opportunity, move us forward, release provision, and more. When we say "Yes" to God, he turns each challenge like a key, allowing it to unlock the favor, resources, and blessings we need to complete our assignment.

The Power of Suffering

Often God uses times of suffering to prepare us for promotion. Joseph, son of Jacob, is a prime example (see Genesis 37, 39–50 for the full story). Joseph's brothers were jealous because he was his father's favorite. Eventually they sold him to traders, then lied to their father and convinced him that Joseph was dead. The traders sold Joseph to a prominent Egyptian named Potiphar, who worked as the captain of Pharaoh's royal guard. Joseph worked at the home of his new boss, and because of his gift of administration and the Lord's favor, everything ran smoothly. Because of God's hand on Joseph, Potiphar began to prosper.

One day Potiphar's wife accused Joseph of rape (falsely), so he was sent to prison. Joseph's ability to manage people brought him favor and he was given authority over the other prisoners. He even used his gift of interpreting dreams to be a blessing to a couple of them as well. I know this story just seems more and more unfair for Joseph, but keep reading.

Two years later a former prisoner remembered Joseph's gift for dream interpretation and mentioned him to Pharaoh, because one night the Egyptian monarch experienced two dreams and they troubled him. Joseph was released from prison and sent to meet with Pharaoh. He correctly interpreted the dreams and provided a wise solution to the problem they foretold. As a result Pharaoh promoted him to the second-highest position in the nation of Egypt.

Joseph was innocent of every accusation along the way, and he certainly didn't deserve to be sold by his brothers. He suffered unjustly for years. At times knowledge of his innocence must have weighed heavily on his mind, but God had a good plan all along. He allowed Joseph's suffering to precede his promotion.

Suffering precedes promotion.

Suffering also teaches us to seek God. In other words suffering teaches us how to pray. Without hardship we have no reason to contend in prayer for answers. Difficulty and delay are often closely related. How often have you been sure your prayer would be answered within a particular time frame? The Old Testament prophet Daniel prayed about a matter for twenty days, but saw no change and received no response to his petition. On the twenty-first day Daniel had a supernatural encounter with an angel who delivered the answer and some long-awaited encouragement (see Daniel 10 for the full story).

How long are you willing to remain steadfast, persistent, and full of faith to see your prayer answered?

Finally, suffering positions us to receive the promises of God. The result of suffering should always be renewed hope. Romans 5:3-5 (NKJV) says: "... but we also glory in tribulations, knowing that tribulation produces perseverance; and perseverance, character; and character, hope. Now hope does not disappoint, because the love of God has been poured out in our hearts by the Holy Spirit who was given to us."

The sacrifice is never greater than the reward—hope does not disappoint.

The Lord is ready to step in and assist us in the midst of our challenges. After all, Psalm 46:1 (NKJV) declares: "God is our refuge and strength, a very present help in trouble."

I heard the following story many years ago, and though I am unsure of its source, it surfaces in my heart whenever I find myself facing a challenge:

A Father's Strength

A young boy and his dad were standing in the backyard one day near a huge rock. The father asked his son, "Do you think you can lift that rock?"

The boy replied, "I'm not sure, but I can try." The boy strained to move the stone, but it simply wouldn't budge.

The father asked, "Son, are you using all your strength?"

"I think I have a little more power," the boy said. He tried again, but the rock still wouldn't move. The boy sat on the stone, sweating, and breathing hard.

"Son, did you use all your strength?" the father asked.

The boy lowered his head in defeat and replied, "Yes, Dad, I used all my strength."

"No, son, you didn't" the father said, "because you never asked for my help."

I hope you will remember this story the next time you face hardship, suffering, or a challenge. Instead of running away, consider standing still and asking God for help. Seeking God's help in prayer is one of the most powerful weapons in your arsenal.

Let's be clear: I can't promise that your difficulties will become painless, nor can I guarantee that things will turn out the way you expect them to. But I do know that your willingness to face difficult situations using God's strength is always the right choice.

It's the right choice for your personal growth and for the people you will influence later. Challenges teach us more than days of smooth sailing ever could. An added benefit is this: as an influencer, the words of encouragement you speak to others will hold more weight when you've lived through what you're talking about. Be encouraged and stay the course. That's how you live out God's assignment for your life.

CHAPTER THREE

GARDENS AND ENEMIES

THE POWER OF OVERCOMING

I was raised in North Carolina. Our home was set on three and a half acres of green grass, bordered by pine trees. We lived on a corner lot, so across the street to the east sat a large cornfield. Across the street to the south was a small farm. My father grew up on a 180-acre farm owned by his father, so I understand why he chose such a rural location to build our home. Although Dad went on to earn a graduate degree in music education and taught for forty years, he never strayed far from his love of the soil. All through my childhood we grew the food we ate. My favorite seasons were spring and summer, mainly because we kept the windows open all over the house. No matter what room you were in, you could smell geranium, freshly cut grass, honeysuckle, and pine wafting in from the yard. At night the crickets and frogs seemed to compete for the most prominent solo, while lightning bugs flashed a counter-rhythm against the night stars.

Plant Villains

My dad loved everything that grew out of the ground, but he focused on our garden and fruit trees while my mom cultivated our flowers. One of the most important things my dad taught me about plants was that each one has a natural enemy, sometimes more than one. He would show me the beetles, aphids, worms, and other creepy-crawlers whose sole purpose was to destroy, consume, or shorten the life of its host plant.

Your enemy will attack what is valuable.

Corn, Worms, and Breath Control

As a kid I was pretty grossed out by bugs, which is unfortunate since one of my chores was to pick corn in summer. I hated the worms I sometimes found when it was time to shuck the corn. I'd hold my breath while removing the outer husks to fully expose the ear, hoping I wouldn't find earworms inside. These pests ate away at everything they touched, so the corn became softened and discolored with decay. I believe the technical term is *yuck*. Whenever I did find damage, my mother would cut away the rotted part without missing a beat, then put the rest of the ear of corn to good use.

Thankfully my father also taught me that a remedy existed for every pest. For example, there are temporary strategies to combat pests, like cultivating ladybugs, which eat earworms. Some farmers use a decoy method: they surround corn with other plants that earworms consume, like lima beans or tomatoes. My father taught me that planting the corn at the wrong time was one of the number one things that made it vulnerable to its natural enemy.

Overcomers Unite

While the solutions I described work to some degree, the deck just seemed stacked against the corn. Year after year the harvest still managed to yield enough to feed our family. The corn example is a good place to start the conversation about an important leadership principle: overcoming.

Overcoming obstacles is a skill all leaders must master.

Facing opposition without quitting helps to mature our leadership gifts. Leaders who use shortcuts or try to bypass challenges may succeed for a while, but in the long run these leaders will lack the fortitude that can only come by enduring hardship.

I've touched on two ideas here:

You will be targeted by the enemy. The problem is, sometimes we are unable to identify his attacks until it is too late. Proverbs 22:3 (MSG) says, "A prudent person sees trouble coming and ducks; a simpleton walks in blindly and is clobbered."

Understand the season you're in. Timing is everything. Ecclesiastics 3:1-3 says, "There is a time for everything, and a season for every activity under the heavens: A time to be born and a time to die, a time to plant and a time to uproot, a time to kill and a time to heal...."

> *Your season of highest use is often preceded by a season of great attack.*

In my work with midshipmen at the Naval Academy, those who have overcome challenges week after week, semester after semester, have encouraged me. I have also been deeply impacted by students who have overcome challenging circumstances before coming to the Academy.

Keep Your Eyes on the Prize

One outstanding overcomer is Marine aviator and motivational speaker Captain Zerbin Singleton. Zerbin was a member of the Gospel Choir and graduated from the Academy in 2008. He was deployed during the writing of this book, but when I emailed him about including his story, he responded quickly and gave me his blessing. I am thankful that he did because his story deeply impacted my life and I hope it will encourage yours.

Born to a drug-addicted mother and abandoned by his father, Zerbin spent his early years in Alaska. He saw unspeakable things as a child and was taken in by family members when his mother faced incarceration. During high school he relocated to Georgia to live with family members. There he excelled in sports and academics, and ultimately graduated as valedictorian of his high-school class. By this time the young man with the unforgiving background had set a goal of becoming an astronaut. He gained admission to the United States Naval Academy, but before beginning his studies, he had a car accident that broke his collarbone and delayed his entry to the Academy by one year. The following year Zerbin enrolled at the Naval Academy and applied himself just as he had in high school. He became an award-winning starter on the Navy football team and gained the respect of his fellow midshipmen. During his senior year Zerbin was named Brigade Commander, which placed him in charge of the entire student body of four thousand midshipmen.

Zerbin's story is nothing short of incredible, and it reminds me of the plants and enemies my father taught me about as a child. Though Zerbin was planted in unfavorable circumstances early in life, he developed the ability to overcome every purpose blocker.

Leaders must overcome every purpose blocker.

He was remarkably clear headed about what he needed to accomplish during his "growth season" at the Academy. I don't think his delayed admission was a coincidence; instead I believe the Lord placed him at the Naval Academy at a specific time in order to accomplish a specific purpose.

Do You See What I See?

I recall hearing a story about a father with twin sons. The father was an abusive, alcoholic man who caused pain and destruction at every turn. One son grew up to be just like him. He was abusive to others, couldn't hold a job, was addicted to alcohol, and brought destruction to everyone and everything he touched. When asked why he lived that way, he answered, "I watched my father."

The other son was a model student and high achiever, and built a stable home for his wife and children. He was a good provider, and known for being kind, loving, and generous. When asked why he lived that way, he answered, "I watched my Father."

While clear perspective, a winning mind-set, and persistence can take the average individual far in life, you'll go even farther when these character traits are rooted and grounded in a relationship with God. Our natural gifts and talents give us clues about our purpose but using our gifts and talents is not enough. Apart from a relationship with God, it isn't possible to fully understand our true identity. (I'll say more about this in an upcoming chapter.)

So keep your eyes on God and live by his Word, and you'll find all the strength and grace you need to overcome anything you face in life!

CHAPTER FOUR

A TALE OF THREE HOUSES

THE POWER OF DETOURS

I grew up in a godly home with my parents and an older brother. My dad became a music teacher during segregation and helped to start the orchestra program at the black schools in my city. After integration he traveled all over the city, teaching music students at several schools each day. My father also sang in the local choral society and played violin in our local symphony for many years. Dad was my first piano and violin teacher, and began training me at about age four. I loved to play the piano, and write songs and sing. Though I played violin until I graduated high school, it never came naturally like piano did.

My mother taught in the fourth grade and was known for running a tight ship. On teacher workdays I would go with her and help grade papers, make photocopies, and change her bulletin boards while she created lesson plans. I always felt sorry for her students because she gave so much homework and taught above grade-level standards. My mother developed a reputation within our school district for getting miraculous results with difficult students. I secretly believe that her high expectations and refusal to accept excuses had a great deal to do with her results.

Though I was a good student, I prayed the entire summer after my third-grade year that I would not get my mother as my fourth-grade teacher. To this day I am convinced that God heard me. Had he not, I might still be completing homework assignments today.

Although my brother and I enjoyed our childhood, my parents expected us to be disciplined and to display a strong work ethic from an early age. I didn't know how much of an asset the problem-solving skills, self-discipline, and confidence would be to me as an adult. Today I am grateful for the time spent doing routine chores, homework and practicing musical instruments, though at the time I thought my parents were way too strict. I had a good childhood, but like most kids I had my share of challenging situations.

Purpose under Attack

In tenth grade I was invited to join the top singing ensemble at my high school. The school was predominately white, but up until that time I hadn't been treated poorly because I was black. Shortly after I joined the singing ensemble, things changed. Late at night students began driving by our home screaming my name, followed by racial slurs, and then they sped away. This happened night after night until my parents became concerned about my safety. Though I never told my parents, one day at school an older, male white student—an athlete as well—pulled me into a secluded area and delivered the same hateful message in person. I've always been quick with words, so I fired off a few choice ones to defend myself. Judging from his raised eyebrows and red face, my verbal slap worked. Shocked, he backed away. Shaken, but physically unharmed, I left that encounter with a pit in my stomach that would remain for many years. That exchange made me fearful and suspicious of southern, white males for a time—after all, before I'd joined the ensemble, that student had always been cordial. Only when I began to succeed did his true feelings become evident. The next year, my parents transferred me to a new school that was more ethnically diverse, and I immediately felt the freedom to pursue my interests without fear.

Looking back, it was the enemy's plan to use that traumatic event to make me unwilling to befriend people outside of my ethnic community, but his scheme didn't work. Had I gone the route the enemy planned for me, the Lord couldn't have trusted me to develop such an ethnically diverse choir decades later. God in his mercy allowed a weapon to be formed against me, but kept it from prospering—just like his Word promises in Isaiah 54:17. The Lord stamped my heart with the pain of that experience, but he also gave me a choice: I could treat others the way I had been treated, or I could become a demonstration of the love of God. By his grace I chose the latter and I have never regretted it.

The enemy of your soul will use pain from the past to try and derail your future.

God Wastes Nothing

The Lord knows how to use every positive encounter and every hardship to accomplish his will. Romans 8:28 says, "And we know that in all things God works for the good of those who love him, who have been called according to his purpose."

I encourage those of you who have lived through difficult childhoods or other hurtful life events to believe that. He is a master at bringing beauty out of ugly moments. Isaiah 61:3 promises that God will allow us to have beauty where there has been destruction and joy instead of sadness. He also promises that we will stand despite all the things that have tried to tear us down.

God gives beauty for ashes, joy for mourning.

Growing up, my brother and I were active at church, school and in the community. My parents encouraged it. They didn't allow us do everything our peers did, but music was one area where they always said, "Yes." As a result my brother and I sang in choirs at school and church, played in orchestras, and appeared on local television shows and I went on to sing in local musical theatre productions. After graduating from high school, my brother chose a military career path and joined the Army. I chose to attend college and study music with a focus on performing and teaching.

Following a Good Example

My mom's example as a teacher and my dad's example as a performing teacher normalized the career path I would eventually take. As it says in Proverbs 22:6 (NKJV), "Train a child up in the way he should go, and when he is old he will not depart from it." This verse was one of my mother's favorite scriptures, and she quoted it often. In college I pursued a degree in classical vocal performance. After graduating I competed in vocal competitions and began to travel across the US and then abroad. I am so thankful for the spiritual and vocational example my parents set. Because of it I was confident about pursuing opportunities to sing.

Ready, Set, Teach

After completing my master's degree in vocal performance, I was hired to teach at Bennett College in Greensboro, North Carolina—following my mother and father into the "schoolhouse" to educate others. I served as Instructor of Music for four years, and when I started, I was only a few years older than my students. I will never forget walking into my first class only to have my students mistake me for one of their peers. When I look back on that first year, I still cringe a little. I had so much to learn. I am convinced that my students taught me more than I taught them, but they survived and so did I.

I did have the common sense to ask my parents how to be a great teacher. I asked both of them to give me the one piece of advice they considered most important.

My father said, "Never, ever, ever give up. Every student is important, and every student can experience success if you stick with it." That advice was deeply personal to him. As a young boy my father had a severe stammering problem. Getting past that impediment had everything to do with people who encouraged him. As he developed confidence, his speech became more fluid. Eventually he went on to talk for a living as a teacher. Even in his later years my father would strike up a conversation with anyone.

My mother's advice was about the mechanics of teaching. She told me that great teachers break complex ideas into small pieces, then they teach those pieces in logical order like building blocks.

Great teachers break complex ideas into small pieces, then connect them like building blocks.

I must tell you, my mother was one of the most brilliant people I have ever known. She was salutatorian of her high-school graduating class at age sixteen, then completed two college degrees with high honors. My parents would often tell the story of how she helped finish my father's master's thesis. Apparently he became so frustrated he wanted to throw the incomplete paper in the nearest river. She simply pointed out the missing elements, developed a strategy and encouraged him to continue.

To this day their advice plays like a recording in my mind at the start of every teaching endeavor. From rehearsals to academic courses and conferences to workshops, I still apply the wisdom they shared.

Armed with good advice and a can-do attitude, I began my teaching career. Little did I know I was about to enter the Holy Spirit's classroom as well. While I learned the ropes as a college instructor, the Lord taught me the value of intercession, fasting, and consistent time in the Word of God. I began to study biblical history and to read the biographies of great men and women of the faith. Though I had always been a dreamer from a child, my dreams and visions increased during this season, and by the time I left Bennett College, I was more spiritually mature and grounded.

Two years into my teaching assignment, I was returning home from Florida after a beach vacation with a friend. As I sat on the plane, I heard the Lord say, "Would you still serve me if the thing you planned to do with your life is not what I am calling you to do right now?" My fear was mirrored in the face of my friend as he grabbed my arm to ask if everything was okay. Things were not okay. I knew that the Lord was asking me to lay aside my pursuit of a performing career, and I didn't want to. I responded in my heart, "Lord, could you repeat the question?" It would be my response for the next two years as I tried to hold onto the dream I had for my life.

I simply could not face the fact that God would ask me to walk away from something I loved so much. As I stubbornly pursued my dream, I watched the favor and opportunities I had become accustomed to in the classical arena begin to disappear, and my time spent in the "opera house" season of my life began to wane.

Will you serve God if it requires you to give up your desires for a season?

No, Not Yet

After a season of resistance, the Lord got my full attention and eventually my obedience. I resigned from my teaching job at Bennett and relocated to the Washington, DC, area. I worked for a few different companies and did ministry work. The Lord used that time to develop my spiritual gifts further and show me my place in the body of Christ. It wasn't exciting or glamorous; most days it felt like a challenging test.

Many moments I longed for my old life of performances, auditions, and travel. I missed the excitement and the money. Even though I'd always been a hard worker, choosing God's path sent me through an intense season of financial hardship—at least that's how I saw it. People who met me during that time never knew the successful college instructor with the promising singing career. They only saw the struggling worship leader with an unfurnished apartment and, for a time, no car. It felt humiliating.

Working as a musician in a church setting had its share of challenges. More than once I saw leaders do things behind the scenes that challenged my faith and saddened me. At the same time, I learned how to listen to the Lord, stay consistent, and avoid ministry pitfalls.

During those difficult years I learned what it meant to live by faith. I also learned the power of giving during a financial crisis.

As the Lord walked me step by step through that
humbling season, things slowly began to turn
around. Soon I had a job in sales, a car, and a fur-
nished apartment. By the time I received word
about the Choir Director position at the Naval
Academy, I was teaching at a private Christian
school and I had a paid church job. More importantly I was submitted to the will of God for my life. He
had been the only constant when my life flipped
upside down, then right side up again. Though I
sang classical music here and there, I was focused
on worship ministry and serving the church—and so
I realized that I had gone from serving in the
schoolhouse to the opera house to the house of God,
all because the Lord knew the plans he had for me
(Jer. 29:11).

Spiritual Boot Camp

As I've explained, the time between leaving my
college teaching position and beginning to work at
the Naval Academy was a spiritual training camp of
sorts. I'm grateful for those years because that's
when I began to apply two principles that I found in
the New Testament:

Becoming all things to all people.

Becoming salt and light.

When the apostle Paul taught about becoming all
things to all men, he wasn't talking about giving up
one's personality. In a real sense Paul was admon-
ishing us to love others. What does that love look

like? Relating to others in ways they can understand and telling the truth (not only the parts they want to hear). As Paul wrote, "I am made all things to all men, that I might by all means save some" (1 Cor. 9:22 KJV).

Further, in Matthew 5, Jesus said:

You are the salt of the earth. But if the salt loses its saltiness, how can it be made salty again? It is no longer good for anything, except to be thrown out and trampled underfoot.

You are the light of the world. A town built on a hill cannot be hidden. Neither do people light a lamp and put it under a bowl. Instead they put it on its stand, and it gives light to everyone in the house. In the same way, let your light shine before others, that they may see your good deeds and glorify your Father in heaven. (Matt. 5:13-16)

We know that salt adds flavor to make food taste better, but it also preserves food and keeps it from decay. Before refrigeration, meat was covered with large quantities of salt and left in a cool place for many days. As the salt drew moisture out of the meat, the waterborne microbes responsible for decay died as well.

How does this apply to leadership?

First, our influence should improve the culture we serve in the same way that salt makes food taste better. Second, just as salt stops decay, our actions, words, and deeds should help slow and even stop the spread of moral decay. When our work environment supports lying or cheating to get ahead, we should choose honesty. When the larger culture says, "Live for yourself," we should serve others first. As we live counter to the culture, some of the people we influence will begin to imitate our example, thereby fighting moral decay.

What about light? Jesus also reminded us that light is meant to shine, not be hidden—highlighting a simple truth:

With leadership comes scrutiny.

When you are a leader, you will not escape being scrutinized and put on display before others, just like a city on a hill. For this reason we need to be cognizant of our choices. With influence comes imitation. If someone imitated everything we did or said, would they be mistaken for a believer?

Salt and Light at the Academy

My spiritual bootcamp years helped me to see salt and light concept in the career opportunities that followed. For example, the Naval Academy mission statement seems to have elements of the "salt and light" principle running through it. The mission of the United States Naval Academy is:

> *To develop Midshipmen morally, mentally and physically and to imbue them with the highest ideals of duty, honor and loyalty in order to graduate leaders who are dedicated to a career of naval service and have potential for future development in mind and character to assume the highest responsibilities of command, citizenship and government.*[11]

With Christ at the center of our life, it is possible to leave situations better than we found them. If we allow him to work in our hearts and lives while we practice patience, he will lead us safely through every detour from one assignment to the next.

[11] "Mission of USNA." The US Naval Academy. Accessed April 1, 2017. https://www.usna.edu/About/mission.php.

CHAPTER FIVE

WITH ONE VOICE

THE POWER OF UNITY

I stood outside the heavy brown door waiting my turn. After glancing at the polished linoleum floor divided into large squares, I shifted my gaze to the concrete wall painted an earthy red. Not my favorite. A quick glance at my cell indicated that I was a few minutes early. I was always a little anxious when I stood there, because it meant that for the next hour I would be exposed to the skill of a vocal surgeon. Instead of a scalpel, she used information. No flaw or imperfection ever escaped her experienced ears. She was unfailingly direct but not unkind. With precision she used her words to carve, chisel, and reshape my voice. The process wasn't physically uncomfortable, but at times it could be emotionally challenging. After years of study I'd disciplined myself to hear her intention without feeling attacked by her critiques.

The door swung open, and two students—likely a singer and pianist—rushed out in a flurry of books, jackets, and hurried good-byes. Their departure revealed the surgeon. Diminutive and a bit stern, she suddenly smiled and stepped aside so I could enter her studio. My nervousness vanished as walked in and got settled. It was time for my weekly voice lesson.

To the left of the door a black grand piano loomed large, and on the wall behind it hung a full-length mirror. Across the room was a large window that looked out on a wide grassy field bordered by trees. Beneath my feet a pale-blue Persian rug covered most of the room's hardwood floor.

My lessons began with a pretty lengthy vocal warm-up to get the breath and voice moving. Once my pianist arrived, I'd sing one piece straight through in performance mode. My teacher would have me sing the piece a second time as she made adjustments to my posture, jaw, tongue, vowel shape, breath, and more.

The technique part of the lesson and the process was full of stops, starts, and spoken commands:

"Jaw straight down—don't jut."

"Go to your body here."

"Stay there—release!"

"What vowel are you singing?"

"Wrong choice, less room, on the staff, please."

If these commands mean nothing to you, don't worry. The important thing is, I understood the technical language and knew what she meant even when I couldn't do it perfectly. The point of the technique lesson was to make micro-adjustments until my voice sounded whole, clear, and powerful from my lowest notes to the highest ones. Classical singing requires a very different approach from the way you'd sing for fun. The classical sound is not necessarily considered beautiful in other genres. As a result, in past decades most classical singers didn't regularly perform jazz, pop, country, or gospel. When they did, they sounded very operatic—an experience that could seem strange or humorous to listeners.

The Sound of Change

In recent years the music industry has changed, as lines between musical styles have become more blurred. Crossover singers like Josh Groban and Andrea Bocelli sing music that satisfies both classical and pop audiences. Some singers don't just cross over; they sing different genres with complete authenticity. Lady Gaga is a fine example of this. On a recent project recorded with the legendary Tony Bennett, she sounds so much like a jazz singer that you'd have a hard time believing she sang pop music.

You may be wondering if any of this has to do with leadership or my time at the Academy. So stay with me here as we move on.

Perception Is Important

When I began working at the Academy, I was leading worship each week in my local church, training worship teams, composing, recording, and teaching music at a private Christian secondary school. Armed with the technique I had learned as a classical singer, I adapted my training to fit each musical setting.

From the beginning I saw how regimented the Naval Academy was. It was a system in which success meant abiding by the rules. As a result, my work there began to feel like a never-ending technique lesson—tedious with little joy. Deep down I wanted to encourage the midshipmen in matters of faith, but things seemed hopeless. I wanted things to operate like crossover singing – displaying the best of both worlds, but I couldn't figure out how. It wasn't until God told me to stay put at the end of my first year that I saw my answer in the most prominent place possible: the Naval Academy mission statement. As we looked at in the last chapter, part of the mission statement reads: "To develop Midshipmen morally, mentally and physically...."[12] There in black and white, I saw how to serve the mission and the midshipmen. I found the crossover.

I would see to it that the Gospel Choir contributed to the *moral* development of the midshipmen in the choir. Instead of asking myself, "How come I

---

[12] "Mission of USNA."

can't talk about God?" I asked, "How do I encourage their moral development by encouraging their faith walk? How do I help them to make right choices? How do I inspire them to choose Christ as their moral compass?"

When the Lord showed me the connection between my life purpose (to serve and influence others for Him) and the Academy mission, I saw how perfect his plans are.

He took this classically trained soprano, derailed my plans, filled me with his Spirit, taught me to lead, then stood me before military officers-in-training from various backgrounds and ethnicities, and asked me to unite them using gospel music—a genre outside my training.

I didn't know his plan when I started, and I had so much to learn, especially about the importance of unity.

All Are Welcome

By my third year I was teaching the Word in small doses and encouraging choir members to get to know the God we were singing about. I am not sure if there was a connection, but from that time onward, students that you wouldn't normally associate with gospel music began to audition for the choir. I never consciously tried to make the choir ethnically diverse; it happened naturally. I'd become so accustomed to studying and performing with musicians from around the world during my days as a classical music student that I never hesitated to allow all midshipmen into the Gospel Choir at the Academy. Like the crossover singers I mentioned earlier, I would be combining people groups and music in new ways.

Once the ethnic diversity of the choir began to change, unity became very important. To me unity means working toward a common goal without discounting anyone. For example each year Gospel Choir has members who excel in meeting academic and athletic standards. These midshipmen willingly mentor and tutor those members who may be less adept at developing strategies for success.

In other words they refuse to leave their shipmates (classmates) behind. True unity makes room for diversity and allows groups to operate from a position of strength.

In a short time two powerful verses from the Bible came alive in our choir:

> You can easily enough see how this kind of thing
> works by looking no further than your own body.
> Your body has many parts—limbs, organs,
> cells—but no matter how many parts you can
> name, you're still one body. It's exactly the same
> with Christ. (1 Cor. 12:12 MSG)

> In Christ's family there can be no division into
> Jew or non-Jew, slave and free, male and female.
> Among us you are all equal. (Gal. 3:28 MSG)

The Membership Process

Membership in the choir is by audition. After a year of accepting midshipmen based on singing ability alone, I learned to expand my criteria a bit. I began to require students to meet high academic standards and to demonstrate spiritual hunger. It took the first four years to get a handle on how to spot students who were strong in all areas. Since freshmen (plebes) had no Academy history, I learned to rely on their performance during plebe summer as well as prayer.

In the beginning I was naïve. I thought that if I prayed and invited the midshipmen who met my criteria, I would have a problem-free choir. After all, these students were the brightest and best, right? Well, I can say this: I have had the pleasure of serving many amazing young leaders, but no choir was free of problems. Many times the Lord did not expose issues or challenges until the fall semester was well underway. I soon realized that the Lord was bringing midshipmen to the choir who needed just as much ministry from God as they would ultimately release *for* God.

The people we lead need as much ministry as they are expected to release.

Some students entered the Academy with a strong faith. Others were babes who had just begun a relationship with God. Still, others had a growing faith – they joined Gospel Choir, then added a campus Bible study or began attending church. Many did not connect deeply with God until after graduation. Whatever the specifics of their spiritual journey, the Lord knew how to use their experiences in Gospel Choir to draw them closer to him. I am grateful that God is faithful to finish what he starts.

God is faithful to finish what He starts.

I told the choir at the beginning of each school year that no one was expected to be the Junior Holy Ghost – in other words no student was expected to be perfect. Instead, all students were encouraged to open their hearts to the Lord. While I often took the liberty of talking about spiritual matters, I was keenly aware that we weren't a church or a Bible study, so I taught the Word in small doses whenever I introduced new songs. I knew that if I did my part, the Lord would reveal himself to my students in his time. My immediate hope was that these principles would be a source of strength and uplift them as they experienced the rigors of Academy life. Whenever I could introduce music that taught forgiveness, love, perseverance, service, unity, and surrender to a mission larger than self, I did. With my long gaze always on unity with God and others, I encouraged connection and a sense of family among the midshipmen in the Gospel Choir.

Gospel Choir as a Cultural Connector

One of the most important lessons I learned in my work at the Academy was the power of connecting disparate cultures. In my experience gospel music is the perfect tool for encouraging unity. Teaching gospel allowed me to share three concepts: culture, music, and the Christian faith.

Each time I explained the text of a new song, I connected it to the Word of God. Each time I taught the music, I talked about the culture that produced the harmonies, rhythms, and style. My process helped students who did not come from an African American background to understand that culture. Why is that important? What benefit could that have for future officers?

It is important to note that the population of the officers-in-training at the Naval Academy, though increasingly diverse, does not yet accurately reflect the demographic of enlisted sailors and Marines. In other words enlisted sailors are largely African American, Latino, and female. When Gospel Choir members graduate and serve as officers, they will carry an awareness of African American culture that may help them to build bridges with the enlisted sailors and Marines they will lead.

Passing the Leadership Test

One of my favorite biblical characters is Daniel of the Old Testament. He stands out to me because of his complete devotion to the God of Israel as a young man. Even after he and his Hebrew companions were taken captive and transplanted to Babylon, given new names, required to master the intricacies of a new culture, and forced to serve a foreign king, Daniel's faith did not falter. After three years of study in a foreign land, Daniel and his companions were required to stand before King Nebuchadnezzar and take a test with many hard questions. If they passed, the king would appoint them to the role of wise men.

Daniel and his friends were determined to keep the laws of their God—the God of Abraham, Isaac, and Jacob. From the beginning of their captivity, they refused to defile themselves by consuming food or drink that had previously been sacrificed to other gods. The decision to put their God first allowed his favor to mark their lives. The Bible declares that when they stood before the king to be tested, Daniel and his friends were ten times wiser than the other wise men, magicians, and sorcerers who served Nebuchadnezzar (see Daniel 1 for the full story).

I believe the Lord showed his favor to Daniel and his friends, causing them to stand out from their peers, because of their unwavering devotion to him. He still does the same thing in the lives of believers today. I see a few parallels to the leadership training at the Academy and the training Daniel had to undergo.

Processed at the Academy

Unlike Daniel, midshipmen come to the Academy willingly after an arduous application process. In similar fashion to Daniel, however, they are quickly separated from all that is familiar, given a new name (number and rank), and required to master a new culture—military culture—complete with its language, customs, and regulations. After three years of training, midshipmen enter their senior (firstie) year with the expectation that they will lead students in junior classes. In this way the fourth year becomes a "test" of the knowledge they have accumulated in the previous years. I have often prayed at the close of our rehearsals that the Lord would be with the members of the Gospel Choir as he was with Daniel, causing them to be ten times wiser than their peers and that he would give them favor with both their subordinates and superiors.

Since beginning with the Gospel Choir in 2006, I had the pleasure of working alongside ten student presidents. Each brought strengths and weaknesses to the task, but one young leader, whom I'll refer to as Midshipman Lewis, stood out in his ability to lead, inspire, and unify others. At the time of this writing, he is serving our nation as a Marine Corps officer. He set a standard of excellence for the choir that not only pleased the Lord, but also gained the notice and appreciation of staff, department heads, and seasoned military officers at the Academy.

Leading Leaders

In late August before his firstie year, Lewis invited me to hear his vision for the choir. As I listened to the presentation, the thought, time, and prayer that had gone into his plans made an impression on my heart. The Holy Spirit was present in that meeting, and I knew I was witnessing something atypical. God had given him a strategy that didn't need adjustments.

His goals were:

To demonstrate the love of God in his service to the choir and to encourage the choir to do the same with one another.

To encourage the choir to demonstrate excellence, unity, and accountability; and to offer rewards for meeting these standards.

He was confident he could meet those goals without compromising military standards. The love and unity that flowed through the choir that year remain a career highlight for me. I believe the Lord honored the vision this young leader set forth because he developed it according to the Word of God. That year taught me a critical lesson:

Effective leaders promote unity; poor leaders encourage division.

Consider four scriptural truths about unity:

Believers should display unity with one another (1 Corinthians 1:10, Colossians 3:13-14, Acts 2:1-4).

Believers are gifted to promote unity (Ephesians 4:11-13, Romans 12:4).

Believers can expect God to provide power that helps them complete tasks assigned by their superiors (2 Chronicles 30:12).

Love is the outward evidence of the presence of unity (1 Peter 3:8).

The scriptures remind us in Psalm 133:1, "How good and pleasant it is when God's people live together in unity!" Yet it might surprise you to know there is unity that God blesses and unity he rejects.

The Unity God Blesses

In the second chapter of Acts, after the ascension of Jesus, we are told that 120 faithful disciples were waiting in an upstairs room in Jerusalem to receive the Comforter promised by Jesus. Their unity pleased God and positioned them to receive the promised Holy Spirit. The same is true today.

Where there is unity, teams can receive blessings and promises from God.

> *Unity positions teams to receive blessings and promises from God.*

At the Academy, unity is integral to leadership development, and the Herndon Monument Climb is a fun yet odd traditional act of unity.

If you've never heard of it, don't worry. Each year the Herndon Monument Climb is the traditional culmination of plebe (freshman) year at the Naval Academy. Demonstrating the teamwork and perseverance that they have learned during their first year at the Academy, the plebe class must scale this obelisk monument by building a human pyramid. Once someone reaches the top, they must remove the plebe cover (hat) and replace it with an upperclassman's cover. Did I mention that tower is covered with vegetable shortening to make the task significantly more difficult? After completing the Herndon climb, the freshmen are no longer called plebes but "fourth class midshipmen."[13] At the Academy, midshipmen are taught to value mission above personal needs and desires. In other words they are always serving an objective that is greater than self.

---

[13] "History and Traditions of the Herndon Monument Climb." The US Naval Academy. Accessed April 1, 2017. https://www.usna.edu/PAO/faq_pages/herndon.php.

A Word of Caution—The Unity God Rejects

Speaking of monuments, the Genesis 11 story of the Tower of Babel recalls an act of human unity that the Lord rejected. At that time all the people on earth spoke the same language. Together they made plans to build a tower whose top would reach the clouds. Not only would this tower be a recognizable landmark, but it would also demonstrate their ability to make a name for themselves—without God. Pride fueled their unity. As a result God confused their language. Once they lost the ability to communicate with one another, they abandoned the work.

God values unity but will never bless human efforts to displace him.

Maybe as you are reading this you consider yourself a believer, but you're trying to build something without seeking God. There is time to change your mind and move in a new direction—his direction. Trust God to give you the plan and a fresh start.

In my time at the Naval Academy, I knew many promising young Christians who placed their desires above God, believing that they could use the same dishonest tactics they saw others using to get ahead. I was heartbroken as I watched some students make choices that cost them their spot at the Academy. Here's the great news: many repented, turned back to God, and moved forward with their lives. In his mercy the Lord allowed them to recover what they lost. He will do the same for you—if you remember the power of walking in the kind of unity that the Lord will bless.

CHAPTER SIX

PRACTICE MAKES PERFECT

THE POWER OF STRATEGY

Growing up, my favorite room at home smelled of lemon furniture polish and books. Every time I walked in, my feet would sink into the carpeting and I'd glance out of the large picture windows. We called that room "the library" because of the books, but it mostly functioned as our music room. It was where my father taught private lessons, and also where my brother and I practiced piano and strings.

Daily I'd make my way to the black padded bench at one end of the room. I would look at the gold letters carved into the wood and read B-A-L-D-W-I-N—the maker of our baby grand piano. With my arms bent in the correct position, my right foot would feel and locate the brass pedals inches above the floor. Carefully I'd arranged my hands on the keys, then begin with a four-octave C major scale. For the next twenty minutes I would practice each scale, leaving the hard ones until the end. For the remaining time I'd play through the pieces I was learning, being careful to observe phrasing and pedal markings as well as fingering suggestions. I loved performing but didn't enjoy the tedious daily practice. Someone once said that scales are to music what grammar is to English, and my father shared that point of view. As much as I disliked them, there was no doubt that mastering the scales improved my playing.

Dad required me to practice piano for an hour each day, but I could usually get away with only a half hour of practice on the violin. It was rare for him to come into the library while I practiced, but I could always tell if he was listening from another room in the house. If I began goofing off or playing a song I had written, he would clear his throat—loudly. That was my cue to get back on track. When I did everything right, he was completely silent or spoke in hushed tones. I was always glad when my practice hour was over.

Practice Makes Perfect

The familiar phrase "Practice makes perfect" is true when it comes to physical and spiritual disciplines. What we practice with our bodies becomes habit due to muscle memory. What we practice spiritually impacts how we live and the people we influence. The truth is, every action we repeat, we will eventually do flawlessly, whether said action is good for us or not.

In the Gospel Choir, I was interested in cultivating natural habits that would promote excellent singing, as well as spiritual habits that would lead to and strengthen my students' relationship with God.

Plant, Water, Increase

In my early years at the Naval Academy, I was very hard on myself because the choir was in a good place musically, but I longed to see greater spiritual growth. I thought it was my responsibility to make each member live for Christ. I was constantly disappointed when I heard testimonies to the contrary. It made me feel as though I wasn't doing enough to show them who Jesus is.

It took me a few years to realize that every midshipman could choose to follow Christ or other paths. In that regard I was grateful for the wisdom found in 1 Corinthians 3:6-8 and Matthew 13:1-23. In the passage from 1 Corinthians, the apostle Paul taught me that God uses more than one person to reveal Jesus:

*Some plant, others water, but God gives
the increase.*

Likewise Matthew 13:1-23 explains how the condition of the heart determines how much insight a person can receive. Sometimes the Word falls on good ground, but it can also fall on shallow ground, stony ground, or thorny ground. The important thing is, God knows exactly which heart attitude every person has. As believers it's our job to keep planting seeds and keep watering the lives of others with love and the Word of God.

Once I began to see that Gospel Choir was just one of the tools God was using to reveal himself to the midshipmen, a greater sense of freedom and confidence entered my heart. Before long I found a balanced way to teach musical and spiritual disciplines in rehearsals without overthinking either.

The Rehearsal Process

I kept Naval Academy Gospel Choir rehearsal simple by design. Academy life is regimented, so predictability makes sense to midshipmen. I quickly learned that in leadership development settings, a lack of structure erodes respect.

In leadership settings, a lack of structure erodes respect.

Each rehearsal began with prayer, followed by physical and sung warm-ups. Next we learned new music or reviewed music from the previous week. If songs required soloists, interested singers auditioned during rehearsal as we went over the song. This could be nerve-wracking for the soloists, but I saw it as an opportunity for midshipmen to conquer their fears. At the end of rehearsal, student or military leadership briefed the choir on important announcements and administrative details. Students then gave praise reports and prayer requests. We prayed, encouraged one another with a hug, and dismissed.

Our rehearsals followed enough structure to meet musical goals but remained elastic enough for the Holy Spirit to comfort, edify, and encourage us. Often when I introduced a song, I could sense the Holy Spirit directing my words, leading me to teach the scriptural principles the song was based on. When I'd pray before arriving at rehearsal, the Holy Spirit would show me specific challenges, strongholds, or areas of discouragement choir members were facing. At some point in the rehearsal, I could always count on him to show me how to speak to those issues.

About the Music

Gospel music is different from other choral music for a few reasons. First its origins are in the folk music of West Africa, which means that one of its underlying functions is to foster community by commenting on daily life – whether that includes faith, celebration or despair. Indeed, this function of singing is common across the continent as noted in *The Awakened Woman* written by Zimbabwean author Dr. Tererai Trent. she writes, "And so we women and girls sit, muscles and tongues loose in the comfort of our togetherness, and, as my people have done for generations, we sing songs and tell stories. As the stories warm our hearts...we are enshrined in a circle of healing."[14] The music continued to carry markers of its origins long after West African music first reached America in the hearts and voices of slaves, after they began to sing hymns from the New World in West African fashion, after hymns gave way to the spiritual, and after spirituals gave birth to blues and jazz, then gospel. Like DNA that marks each member of a family, traces of West African culture have remained a part of the essence of gospel music.

The role composed music plays in western European culture has some fundamental differences. While some European folk music exists to accompany life moments, serious European composers sought to display technical skill and virtuosity. These characteristics defined musical beauty and importance in European culture. A notable exception is opera, which is built on stories that mirror the full range of human experiences. For the most part, western European musical composition is produced to thrill the heart musically and lyrically while fo-

---

[14] Trent, Tererai. *The Awakened Woman.* New York, NY: Enliven/Simon and Schuster, 2017, 2.

cusing on lofty and at time esoteric themes. It also requires two distinct groups: audience and performer.

Music of the African diaspora especially gospel, is quite different. In part, it exists to unite a community by repeating truth or emotion until everyone joins on one accord.[15] There are no silent listeners – all participate. A second distinction is that gospel music uses "call-and-response" as the primary means of teaching and performing. As its name suggests, call-and-response indicates repetition of a musical phrase between a leader and a group of singers. Gospel choirs do not read music scores; they read the gestures of the director. A gospel choir director uses hand gestures that are quite different from those in other choral styles. With a few simple signals a gospel director can indicate what section of the song the choir should sing, which harmonies should be sung, in what order, and for how long. Singers who come from a music-reading background often experience a learning curve as they adjust to the rote learning and gesture-based direction.[16]

In addition to the difference in teaching style, gospel music is always paired with dance. At the Academy, I used a simple but effective method to get all singers on the same musical and spiritual page despite skill level, ethnicity, or level of faith.

---

[15] Scott, *Gospel Music Training*, 22-46.
[16] Scott, *Gospel Music Training*, 22-46.

First Physical, Then Vocal

After opening prayer came a physical warm-up that could include shoulder rolls, stretching the arms over head, toe touches, and other gentle movements to get the body warm and pliable. Next I often used line-massage as a way to create a connection between members while relieving the upper back tension that can result from sitting through hours of classes.

After all of this, the choir was ready to sing. I started with a simple polyphonic song accompanied by the band. Poly-phonic simply means "many sounds' in this case, a chorus with a different melodic line for each voice part. I also chose a chorus that was easy to sing while changing keys by half steps, allowing me to combine warm-ups with ear training. Following warm-ups, we worked on actual songs.

Keep it Moving

Since most midshipmen do not attend the Academy to pursue a musical career, I created an environment where average singers could produce above-average results. Critical, humorless rehearsals may pull the best out of gifted solo artists, but average singers require a balance of encouragement and critique.

Choir Time Is Family Time

By the start of my third year at the Academy, I noticed that choir members began to refer to themselves as "family." Midshipmen from all classes interacted with one another, providing spiritual, academic, and athletic support. In Academy culture, unity across class lines is not always encouraged due to distinctions in rank. Each class has a bit more responsibility and authority than the classes below them.

Although student rank was recognized and respected within Gospel Choir structure, this did not prevent the choir from functioning as a connected, unified whole.

Teaching More than Music

In addition to teaching music, I also developed a few spiritual lessons that I would teach each year. I taught these concepts because of the impact they had on midshipmen as believers and as future officers. The Lord encouraged me to speak directly to real-life issues like integrity, sexual purity, delayed gratification, the power of suffering, how to manage challenges/challenging people, and much more. One topic I addressed every year without fail was unforgiveness.

Learning to forgive is vital to good leadership.

It has been my observation that God allows leaders to endure tremendous hardship, almost like a plant fighting its way through rocky soil to expose itself to fresh air and sunlight. Some leaders learn to out-perform their pain, and at the Naval Academy, performance is highly encouraged. Even leaders who do a good job of masking their pain leave signs that something is amiss, as people who have unresolved pain and un-forgiveness tend to display bitterness.

Over the years midshipmen in the choir spoke with me privately about family members or friends they just couldn't seem to forgive. I considered these moments of transparency an act of tremendous bravery, because in a military environment such vulnerability can come across as weakness. For this reason students have to be wise about how and to whom they disclose personal trials. Disclosures about painful situations became so frequent that I asked the Lord to give me a way to address it.

He gave me the following demonstration: I often asked two students—we'll call them A and B—to link arms. Student A represented an unforgiving person while student B represented the person or situation they were having trouble forgiving. Once their arms interlocked, I told them that refusing to forgive is like choosing to hold the worst moments of your life in a tight embrace forever.

Refusing to forgive is like choosing to hold the worst moments of your life in a tight embrace forever.

As students A and B began to walk around the room linked together, everyone could see the powerful visual: until we forgive, we carry the horrible incident, wound, or person with us constantly. The moment we forgive, however, we will disengage from that person or situation and if we seek him, connect to God who will begin to heal the wounds in our souls.

Acts 3:19 says, "Repent, then, and turn to God, so that your sins may be wiped out, that times of refreshing may come from the Lord."

It is not easy to let go of past hurts. Our wounded soul rehearses each painful encounter over and over again until we put a stop to that cycle in prayer. Here's the truth: in this life, betrayal, hurt, and abuse will visit each of us. What we do with that pain is up to us. The leader who masters forgiveness and release will become a force to be reckoned with.

A Testimony of Forgiveness

After teaching the forgiveness illustration one year, a choir member I'll call David approached me. He was one of the most humble yet high-achieving students at the Academy. A leader among leaders, recipient of prestigious awards and honors, he was growing rapidly in his walk with God. Part of his determination to succeed was no doubt driven by the scars from a tough childhood. For all the progress he was making in the right direction at the Academy, I could see that his heart was heavy about something.

He talked openly about the un-forgiveness he harbored against a family member. As he poured out his heart, the Holy Spirit unveiled a strategy to me. I told David to write a letter of honor to this family member and thank them for every good thing they had done for him over the course of their relationship. I told David to apologize for anything he himself had said or done to harm the family member. In just a few short weeks David pulled me aside with a praise report. He let me know that while things were not perfect, they were better than they had been in a long time between himself and the family member. He thanked me for the counsel and lesson on forgiveness.

Humbling ourselves, especially when we have every reason to be angry, is a tall order. If we can just learn to trust God even when his ways seem counterintuitive, He will change us or our situation for the better.

Another spiritual concept I emphasized in Gospel Choir was trusting God to deliverer us when we are in trouble, because I wanted my students to understand that God is faithful and powerful.

Two testimonies stand out when I think about the delivering power of God. In both I marvel at the way midshipmen continued to trust God while enduring rough moments.

What If They Harm Me?

In the first instance one midshipman was a victim of a violent attack at an off-campus event. The student went through the proper legal channels and ultimately saw justice served, but the process took an entire school year. During that time I watched this midshipman faithfully attend choir rehearsals— sometimes worshipping, at other times weeping, and occasionally I saw a smile or two—but no matter their emotional state, this midshipman kept showing up. Months later I heard the horrific details of the attack, which broke my heart and made me furious at the same time. I prayed and sent the following note:

> I just found out about [everything] last night after choir rehearsal. It hurts me to see you walk through something so painful. Please know that I am praying for you, pulling for you, and that I believe in you!!!

> I will be praying that justice is done, that you are healed and restored, and that God turns this around for you while everyone, including the enemy, watches. You are so much more than the

lies that come out of the enemy's mouth. You will NEVER be forsaken by God, or us!

Much love, unceasing prayers ...

Sometime later the student responded:

Ms. Scott,

Thank you very much for your encouraging words and prayers. I find that sometimes when I look back, and I have no clue how I stand here today. [I know] that it's nothing that I am even remotely deserving of. I know that there are a lot of people out there that truly love me and most importantly I know there is a higher power that has his hand on me.

This student's resolve to worship through that trial was sobering. When they missed a rehearsal, I prayed fervently. When they attended rehearsal, I stood in awe of God's strength at work.

My intention was not only to teach music, but also to encourage midshipmen to draw close to the God we sing about. I wanted them to believe that He would hold them and fight for them no matter how difficult times got.

God the Healer

I vividly remember the second instance. During that semester one of the choir's most exuberant members shared a prayer request about a family member with cancer. Over the following weeks we continued to keep their family in prayer, until one night the Lord led me to ask the choir to make a declaration that the family member would be cancer free. As the choir prayed, there was a very unusual release of the Spirit of God. I could sense something break in the spirit realm. By the end of that semester, not only was the student's family member given a remission report, but they also attended their first choir concert in over a year, rejoicing all the way. It was wonderful for all of us to see the result of God's faithfulness, and to experience his willingness to hear and answer our prayers for healing.

It's true that strategic practice makes perfect, whether we're practicing scales and songs or forgiveness and faith. It is also important for leaders to remember that what we practice in public and in private has the power to impact the people we serve. While it is an honor to influence others, we also have a responsibility to be strategic in our personal lives by staying in right standing with God so that we do not become a stumbling block to those who look to us for guidance and direction.

CHAPTER SEVEN

THE EVERYTHING BAGEL

THE POWER OF DIVERSITY

In the blissful years before carbohydrates became my enemy, I often ate plain, toasted bagels with cream cheese for breakfast. On days when I wanted something especially decadent, I'd have a plain toasted bagel with butter and crispy bacon. While in the deli, I often took note of the other bagels available. Although I had never eaten one, the "everything bagel" always stood out to me. Heavily caked with various seeds and bits of onion, salt, and garlic, I found its appearance overwhelming. There were simply too many things going on. I was perfectly fine with my plain bagel. There were no surprises in taste or texture. It was easy to eat and even easier to forget. What's not to love? I want to you to remember my initial thoughts about that everything bagel, because time has a way of changing both our perceptions and desires.

You may be wondering what bagels and a military gospel choir have in common, and I will get to that, but first let me take a brief detour and explain why gospel choirs exist at US colleges in the first place.

In the 1970s in the United States, the black community experienced a resurgence rivaling that of the 1920s Harlem Renaissance. Blacks celebrated and studied the West African history lost to us as a result of slavery. The "black is beautiful" and "black pride" movements that started in the 1960s reached their culmination in the 1970s. The confidence and unity these movements inspired within the black community became a phenomenon that made its way around the world in part through the writings of Steven Biko on the African continent; the wearing of the afro hairstyle in the US, South America, and the Caribbean;[17] and through the international spread of black music, including gospel.

No longer confined to the church, gospel music was heard on secular radio and appeared in recordings, films, on Broadway, and in the most prestigious concert halls in the world. The well-known artist Mahalia Jackson performed at the request of the queen of England, while a young gospel singer from California named Andraé Crouch sang at the White House for Naval Academy alumnus and then President Jimmy Carter. Carter had been a

---

[17] "Black is beautiful." Wikipedia. Accessed August 14, 2017. https://en.wikipedia.org/wiki/Black_is_beautiful.

classmate and close friend of the Academy's first African American graduate, Wesley Brown, whom we looked at earlier.

The immense popularity of gospel music across the United States, and in countries around the world, caused choirs to spring up on most American college campuses during the 1970s. Although an authorized gospel choir was not formed at the US Naval Academy until the 1980s, its appearance was no doubt influenced by the events of previous decade. In fact, during the early '70s, several black male midshipmen started a gospel ensemble called "Upper Room." They experienced short-lived success but were never granted official club status on campus.[18]

A decade later in February 1985, West Point's Cadet Gospel Choir visited the US Naval Academy to perform during a Black History Month chapel service. That visit galvanized black midshipmen, who immediately formed a student-led USNA Gospel Choir. They secured then LT Laura Stubbs, a black female engineering professor, to oversee, direct, and accompany them on piano. Through her efforts the Gospel Choir gained traction and received a student activities charter. Dr. Barry Talley (then Director of Musical Activities) formulated a plan to give the choir structure, its operating budget and a professional director.[19]

[18] Scott, *Gospel Music Training*, 55

[19] Scott, *Gospel Music Training*, 55.

The director he chose was Mrs. Joyce Garrett, who was then and still remains well-known in the Washington, DC, area. With two earned degrees in choral conducting, Garrett had achieved international notoriety for her work. In 1988, Garrett entered her students from Eastern High School in a choral competition in Vienna, Austria. Out of eight international finalists, they earned second-place honors.[20] When Garrett returned to the US, she received engagement offers from the White House, Kennedy Center, and other high-profile opportunities. At one of those Kennedy Center performances in 1989, Barry Talley, who brought the Naval Academy Men's Glee Club to the same event, heard Garrett's choir. He subsequently offered her a job directing the Gospel Choir at the US Naval Academy, and she accepted.

When Mrs. Garrett resigned in 2006, I was hired to direct the choir. The group I inherited was largely African American, but within the first several years that began to change. I never listened to anyone who advised me to limit the ethnic diversity of the choir. Later I'll discuss how important that decision was.

Now back to those bagels.

---

[20] Ron Arias and Chris Phillips, "Choir Director Joyce Garrett Battles D.C.'s Mean Streets with the Power of Positive Singing," *People*, June 12, 1989. Accessed April 1, 2017. http://people.com/archive/choir-director-joyce-garrett-battles-d-c-s-mean-streets-with-the-power-of-positive-singing-vol-31-no-23/.

For its first seventeen years the Gospel Choir was like a plain bagel. Due to the historical reasons I've discussed, the choir comprised mainly African American students. I see this as a blessing and an important reflection of events in American history. The Gospel Choir began as one of the few expressions of African American culture at the Academy and its existence encouraged and grounded the midshipmen it served.

First Corinthians 15:46 says that natural things precede spiritual things. Mrs. Garrett's primary task was to raise the performance level of the choir, and to establish a solid musical foundation and organizational infrastructure while providing a meaningful outlet for the small number of African American students enrolled at the Academy at the time. Over a decade after her departure, the choir stands on the foundation she built of encouraging high musical standards.

I became Gospel Choir director at a time when the Naval Academy population was becoming more diverse than ever. Although ethnic diversity had increased on campus, minority students are still a small part of the overall student body. To bond with other minorities, many of these midshipmen found a home in the Gospel Choir.

Just like the everything bagel that I discussed earlier, by 2009 students from various ethnic backgrounds, denominations, and musical experiences soon constituted the choir. Instead of feeling overwhelming, it was wonderful. In fact, around the same time, the word *diversity* was gaining tremendous momentum at American universities.

In 2006, Walter Benn Michaels, professor of English at the University of Illinois—Chicago, wrote the scholarly article, "The Trouble with Diversity." The article has been expanded into a book, but in the original essay he discussed the growing attention paid to diversity as an idea that "emerged out of the struggle against racism."[21] To make his argument, he cited the 1978 Bakke v. Board of Regents ruling that made racial diversity an acceptable goal for a university admissions policy.

The United States military was also conducting diversity research. In 2009 retired Air Force General Lester Lyles was appointed to serve as Chairman of the Military Leadership Diversity Commission. This commission was established by the National Defense Authorization Act, and it comprised retired and active-duty military officers, senior enlisted, corporate executives, civil servants, and a law school chancellor. It was formed to research and recommend "policies and practices to help develop future military leaders who represent … America."[22]

---

[21] Walter Benn Michaels, "The Trouble With Diversity," *The American Prospect*, Aug. 13, 2006. Accessed May 12, 2017. http://prospect.org/article/trouble-diversity.

[22] Lester L. Lyles, *From Representation to Inclusion: Diversity Leadership for the 21st-Century Military*, Military Leadership Diversity Commission, March 15, 2011. Accessed May 5, 2017. https://www.hsdl.org/?view&did=11390, viii.

When the commission issued its final report of findings in 2011, it stated:

> The Armed Forces have not yet succeeded in developing a continuing stream of leaders who are as demographically diverse as the Nation they serve. Current projections suggest that the proportion of racial/ethnic minority youth will increase in this century, while the proportion of non-Hispanic white youth will decline. More importantly, racial/ethnic minorities and women are still underrepresented among the Armed Forces' top leadership, compared with the service members they lead.[23]

I was connected to this national discourse on diversity because of the ethnic makeup of the Gospel Choir. During most of my tenure, our group played a significant role in Naval Academy efforts to recruit minority high school candidates. Our musical tours were planned and funded by the Admissions Department with outreach goals in mind, and increased in size and scope during my decade with the choir. By 2011, I began to receive positive feedback from senior leaders at the Academy. Whenever officers—active or retired—would attend performances or rehearsals, aside from enjoying the performance, they commented on two things:

---

[23] Lyles, *From Representation to Inclusion*, xiii.

How well the diversity in the Gospel Choir reflected the diversity in the fleet.

How the choir appeared to be the most diverse student group on campus.

In hindsight, by encouraging ethnic diversity within the Gospel Choir, I unknowingly positioned it to serve the recommendations of the Military Leadership Diversity Commission—an organization that I didn't even know existed until I began writing this book. Through it all, the Gospel Choir provided a place for midshipmen to unite with one another and express a common faith in song while carrying out the goals and aims of the Naval Academy mission.

CHAPTER EIGHT

WHO ARE YOU?

THE POWER OF IDENTITY

In 2012, a week before the Gospel Choir was scheduled to travel to Atlanta, Georgia, over the Martin Luther King Jr. holiday, I received a call from Zion Baptist Church in DC, where I served as worship leader. The pastor informed me that President Barack Obama and the First Family would attend Zion that Sunday in celebration of Martin Luther King Jr. Day. I contacted my boss at the Naval Academy to inform him. He reasoned that the Commander in Chief was everyone's boss at the Academy, so I should go and sing.

I told the choir and musicians that I'd be leaving the tour early, but I didn't explain the details until the Saturday I departed. Keeping the secret led to hilarious speculations on the part of the midshipmen. Some thought I was eloping with a famous man. Others assumed I was going to pick up a rare dog from a breeder. A few even imagined I had adopted a child from a foreign country. Their explanations for my departure were so exciting and adventurous that I hoped my news wouldn't be anti-climactic. I shouldn't have worried. They were overjoyed and erupted into shouts and applause when I told them. I asked for their prayers and hurried to catch my flight from Atlanta to Baltimore.

For the church staff, Sunday morning began very early with detailed instructions from the Secret Service. We were told where to stand, what to do, and what to avoid, including reminders not to approach the POTUS or the First Family, and to refrain from taking photos. I remember a sobering moment when the security team used a dark material to cover all windows that might provide a sightline between photographers—or people with worse intentions positioned outside, and the First Family.

The service began in the typical fashion, except that the sanctuary was at capacity. I wasn't nervous or overly focused on our special guests. That morning before I'd arrived at church, I asked the Lord to be present in a powerful way and to give me a song list that would encourage the congregation to lift their voices in praise.

The First Family filed in just before praise and worship began, and they participated fully in the service. After leading worship I saw that there were no seats left in the musicians' section of the platform, so I stood by the exit. Trying not to be obvious, I glanced at the Obamas from time to time and was struck by the easy dynamic between the President and First Lady. She was bubbly, energetic, and full of life. He on the other hand seemed steady and reserved. After the sermon came a closing prayer. I bowed my head, but in my peripheral vision, I saw the door swing open next to me. In a moment of panic, I realized the First Family would probably leave the sanctuary during the prayer—and walk just inches from where I stood! My heart pounded, and I felt both trapped and excited.

I continued to look down, then saw a hand extend itself toward me. When I looked up, there stood First Lady Michelle Obama. She embraced me and said kind things about the worship set. Although we were the same height, about five-ten, she was much thinner in person than she appeared on television. I resumed my prayer posture, but then another hand appeared—this time belonging to President Barack Obama. He too embraced me and thanked me for the worship songs. Their daughters filed out behind their parents, and I remember a young Sasha looking back at me several times as her family disappeared around the corner.

God arranged that and other moments I've experienced with great men and women based on his Word. Proverbs 18:16 (NKJV) says, "A man's gift makes room for him, and brings him before great men." Since it was part of God's plan for using the gifts he'd given me, every detail had fallen into place. From gaining the permission of my boss and leaving Atlanta early, to being assigned to Zion Baptist as its worship leader, I didn't need a strategy; I simply needed to obey the Lord. God arranged things just like he promised in Psalm 139:16 (NLT):

"Every day of my life was recorded in your book. Every moment was laid out before a single day had passed."

I share all this to encourage you that your steps have been ordered by God. Remember this: plans change, but purpose is constant.

Plans change, but purpose is constant.

The opportunity to minister to our Commander in Chief and his family was a moment that I knew God was orchestrating as it was happening. There are other encounters, however, that only make sense in hindsight.

Disruptions, Changes, and New Territory

For example I can remember the exact season the Lord reordered my steps to Annapolis, Maryland, home of the Naval Academy. I had lived in the DMV area (DC, Maryland, Virginia) for years, but I had never been interested in the bayside town. Suddenly, a year before the choir director position became available, I started taking nightly drives to Annapolis. I couldn't believe how beautiful it was. My first visit hooked me. I was drawn to explore every nook and cranny of Annapolis, and after every visit it felt more and more like my secret getaway. On my drives I found myself at peace, charmed by the area's neighborhoods, waterways, and quiet atmosphere. I took an evening drive several nights a week for about three months, but as my life grew busier, I stopped. I had no clue that in less than a year, God would call me to serve him there.

Three of my biblical heroes had similar experiences that involved relocation: Abraham, David, and Abigail.

In Genesis 12:1 (KJV), God told Abraham, "Get thee out of thy country, and from thy kindred, and from thy father's house, unto a land that I will shew thee." Abraham obeyed the Lord and physically moved to an unfamiliar country before the will of God became evident to him.

Annapolis was unfamiliar territory to me until God placed a desire within me to visit it frequently. Once I did, I began to imagine myself buying a home there. God had something else in mind, though—my next assignment.

Next, as we looked at earlier, God anointed David to be king years before he actually sat on the throne to rule. To prepare him, God took the lowly shepherd boy from the fields and sent him to the palace to work as a musician (see 1 Samuel 16:14-23 for the full story).

Finally, Abigail moved from her home to the palace where she became one of King David's wives. Her transition began when she saved her household from destruction after her husband, Nabal, refused to show hospitality to David and his men. Nabal had enjoyed the protection of David's warriors, and though he was a wealthy man, he was too selfish to provide them a simple meal in return. Abigail disarmed David's anger by speaking words of apology and wisdom, and by providing food for his troops. After Nabal died, David remembered Abigail and asked her to become his wife (see 1 Samuel 25 for the full story).

Someone reading this needs to know that the Lord can take you from the shadows to the spotlight whenever he gets ready. It doesn't matter what others think or see when they look at you. God looks at your heart—and he knows what he has created you to accomplish. Never be discouraged when others overlook you. It is often God's way to hide you and protect the gifts you carry until the time is right for him to display them.

First Learn, Then Rule

Although David eventually became king of Israel, his first visit to the palace wasn't so he could become a ruler; it was so *he could learn about ruling*. I wonder, how many of us will remain humble, and endure jealousy, personal attacks, and frustration like David did as he allowed the Lord to prepare him to reign?

Waiting is one of the most powerful preparatory tools God uses. In my own life after seasons of waiting, God anointed me to function as a leader of leaders at the Naval Academy, to sing and speak on stages around the world, to write the book you are reading now, and so much more. My assignments have been preceded by spiritual battles, tests, and moments of being overlooked. Every challenge has been a blessing in disguise because God used each one to refine me. Every victory is like a crown that I willingly give back to the Lord. He alone deserves the glory.

My time at the Naval Academy was not the culmination of my life's purpose. Instead it was a time of preparation for my next season.

Look for Disruptions and Interruptions

Look around you. Is the Lord leading you into unfamiliar territory? Is anything new or unusual? Are there disruptions to your routine? Pay attention and let God point you in the direction of your next assignment. Interruptions take many forms remember, for Queen Esther, it was a beauty contest; for Ruth, Abraham, and Moses, it was a geographical relocation; for David, it was playing his harp for the king; and for Abigail, it was becoming the wife of a fugitive warrior and future king.

As you read this, you may be feeling forgotten and wondering if your life matters. You may have had high hopes and big dreams that haven't worked out as you planned. You may wonder if you are destined to do something greater in life that impacts others positively. You may be approaching a life transition, such as graduation, accepting a new position, or changing careers. You might be a parent, entrepreneur, public servant, or pastor.

Wherever you find yourself in life, please know that God will move heaven, earth, people, and circumstances to make sure you connect to the assignments and plans he has for your life. Jeremiah 29:11 says, "'I know the plans I have for you,' declares the LORD, 'plans to prosper you and not to harm you, plans to give you hope and a future.'"

True Identity

Inside the heart of all influencers lives an important question. It has been entered into Google searches more than one billion times as I am writing this book. I was stunned when I saw it. The question is: "Do I matter?"

If we observe American culture, we see people of all ages attempting to answer, "Do I matter?" by trying to gain the approval and recognition of others. The truth is, all of us want to be known and loved. We want to know that we are here on this earth for a reason. We want to leave an impact. That desire is a great equalizer. No one is immune. At one time or another, everyone struggles with questions of self-worth and value.

The answer to the question "Do I matter?" according to God's Word is a resounding "YES!" The problem is that this doesn't always feel true.

What Is Community?

Consider that around forty years ago almost everyone knew their neighbors by name and participated to some degree in local government meetings, church services, and other community-based events.[24] Today's society poses a stark contrast. As the internet and social media have gained traction, the word *community* has become a broad term referring to the virtual friends we choose to relate to instead of our neighbors next door or the grocer down the block.

Identity and Isolation

Eileen E.S. Bjornstrom, from the University of Missouri, published a relevant 2011 study in the journal of *Social Science & Medicine.* The study "found that people who said they knew and trusted their neighbors were also more likely to report higher rates of health and well-being than those who did not know or trust their neighbors."[25]

In other words disconnection from each other can cause us to question our value in this world.

"Do I matter?" points to an identity crisis. Can we know who we are without knowing God? Per-

[24] Melissa Dahl, "A Third of Americans Have Never Met Their Neighbors," NYMag.com: Science of Us, Aug. 24, 2015. Accessed April 26, 2017. http://nymag.com/scienceofus/2015/08/third-of-americans-dont-know-their-neighbors.html.
[25] Dahl, "A Third of Americans."

sonally I don't think so. We can know who our friends and family think we are. We can know who society says we are. We can even decide for ourselves who we are. The question is, how do we know when we've gotten these assessments right? What's the standard? Personal comfort? Money? A life without problems?

Senate Chaplain and retired Admiral Barry Black wrote: "Wise people pursue God, for He alone can fill the void within us. Looking for satisfaction without the divine factor is futile, for God has made us for Himself."[26]

Our identity cannot be fully known until we know our Creator. We were made for him.

While some people may disagree with me, I am certain that God is real. He has power beyond human power and He is the reason for our existence. Understanding who we are and why we exist requires us to acknowledge and submit to God.

---

[26] Barry C. Black, *From the Hood to the Hill: A Story of Overcoming* (Nashville, TN: Nelson, 2006), 119.

Out of Step with God

How do we make room for God when doing so is counterintuitive to what our culture says? More importantly, why should we acknowledge God at all?

First, if we don't acknowledge God, we will replace him with self. Our highest goals will become self-love, self-worship, self-importance, and self-affirmation.

Whatever good we say or think about ourselves should be rooted in what God has to say about us. Believe me, you can't come up with more incredible things to say about yourself than what God has already declared about you. Want to know a secret? He has the power to make what he says a reality—us and our promises, not so much. I have good news: you don't have stay on the self-worth treadmill of telling yourself how wonderful you are one minute but not believing it the next. You don't have to indulge every desire that comes to mind to prove your worth or to love yourself. First things first. Get clear about who God says you are. But how do you know if you are thinking clearly about your identity?

The Importance of Clarity

A departure from clear thinking about our identity has consequences. Forgetting God places pressure on us that we were never meant to withstand. When we forget God, we become self-focused and less empathetic to others. Eventually our hearts become hardened toward God. Instead of relying on him and turning to his Word and prayer for answers, we look to the wisdom of men, the culture, and ourselves. Instead of losing interest in bad or destructive habits, we engage in them more and more. Instead of being sensitive to the voice of God, we mock or even curse those who speak for him.

Just scroll through the comments section of any social media post and you'll see what I mean. Comments from one stranger to another range from mean-spirited to violent. Continue reading comments and you'll begin asking, "What happened to common decency?" or "Where is the love?" The Word declares that God is love. It is an unchanging truth that constitutes his nature.

I believe we have lost sight of the God of love, who is our moral compass and North Star. Just a few decades ago, even unbelievers knew this much. Today, our self-centered mindsets have created a vicious cycle; when we leave God out of the picture, we're left hopeless, filled to the brim with self-worship, yet clueless about real love. The remedy is found in understanding what God has to say about us.

What Does God Think of Me?

I want to assure you that God loves you and thinks highly of you. He has a good plan for every human that has ever existed or will ever exist. The scriptures tell us that we were created for relation-ship with God and to demonstrate his glory. We are supposed to know him and display his goodness everywhere we go.

When sin destroyed our ability to connect to God, he sent his Son Jesus to earth to live as a hu-man like one of us. The big difference: Jesus never sinned. Instead he died on a cross to pay the penalty for our sins. Then he was raised from the dead. Now if this sounds like the best action movie you've ever seen, believe me, it's better than that.

When Jesus completed his mission, he was given authority by God to act as the bridge or "way" for each of us to be reconnected with God the Father without our sin blocking the way.

Another way of seeing salvation is this:

From Law Breaker to Model Citizen

Let's say you broke the law by stealing or com-mitting a violent crime and were arrested. You'd probably hire an attorney to lessen or escape your charges. So you walk into the courtroom with a well-prepared lawyer who argues your case, but the judge remains unmoved and proclaims you guilty.

Now imagine a man walking into that same courtroom during your trial—a man who has noth-ing to do with your crime. He offers to take your charges and your place in jail, pay your fine, and even take the death penalty if that is what it will take to free you.

To your surprise the judge agrees to sentence the innocent man and drops all charges against you. In the eyes of the law, it's as though you never did the crime and you escape all punishment.

That is what Jesus's life, death, burial, and resurrection did for us. When we accept his payment for our sins, God drops all the charges against us. Instead of being our Judge, he becomes our Friend.

Maybe you think a leadership book is a peculiar place to talk about salvation. You might also think it strange to pray while reading a book, but if you've never accepted Jesus as your Savior, now is your chance. Simply pray this prayer:

Lord Jesus, I have said, done, and thought things that displease you, and I'm sorry. Today I surrender my life to you. I believe that you are God and that you came to earth, lived as a man, died, and rose again to pay the price for my sins. I accept your gift and I give you my life. Lord, send your Spirit to teach me how to live for you. In Jesus's name, amen.

If you prayed that prayer, I want to encourage you to find a Bible teaching, Bible believing church in your area and begin going! If you're not sure how to find one, ask the believers you work with or the members of your family who attend church. And remember that once you know you are God's friend, your identity becomes every good thing his Word says about you!

CHAPTER NINE

CONQUER FEAR, ACT IN FAITH

THE POWER OF FAITH

I am normally able to control my nerves pretty well before singing. Maybe that's because I have performed for so long that I think of jitters and butterflies as a conversation between body and brain. The butterflies are my brain telling my body to prepare to do something out of the ordinary. My body responds by "revving its engines," so to speak. Nerves can show up as a rapid heartbeat, sweaty palms, or dry mouth. As soon as the performance starts, however, that conversation between body and brain stops, and suddenly the anointing, muscle memory, and my mind synch up to help me communicate a message.

I've had two performances that made me unusually nervous. The first time was when I sang the South African national anthem for President Nelson Mandela, and the second was my first performance on a Kennedy Center main stage. Ironically I did both performances with my longtime voice teacher at her generous invitation. We love singing together, and we performed a cappella duets on both occasions.

The first instance was in November of 2001. President Mandela was to be the keynote speaker at the Anwar Sadat Lecture for Peace at the University of Maryland, my alma mater. I wasn't as nervous about singing for him so much as I was about singing the words correctly in the Xhosa language. Thankfully our performance went well. When President Mandela walked out onto the platform, it felt as if a wave of love accompanied him that charged the atmosphere. I have never experienced anything like it before or since. It was as though the compassion he carried spilled over and filled the room, where an estimated ten thousand people waited to hear him speak.

In the second instance at the Kennedy Center, I was performing with my teacher for a benefit concert to raise money for scholarship students like I had been. I wasn't nervous until after the performance ended when it became obvious that by inviting me to sing, she had offended another faculty member. I remember knots forming in my stomach as I listened to my teacher and the professor shout at one another in the hallway outside the green room. The joy I'd experienced in the performance quickly turned to nausea and anxiety.

The opposing professor thought it was unfair to give me an opportunity to sing at the Kennedy Center when no other faculty performer had included a student. My teacher, on the other hand, didn't see how the professor's opinion was her problem. Further she believed that if donors heard what scholarship students could do, it would motivate them to continue supporting the program.

In the end my teacher's logic won, and a few days later the opposing professor wrote me a letter of apology. Also, the glowing *Washington Post* review we received the next day was a nice confirmation of my teacher's choice. Going forward, other professors began to include scholarship students for that concert, so I am glad that my momentary discomfort benefitted others.

Most of us have experienced the anxiety that accompanies doing something new. From riding a roller coaster to public speaking to applying for a new job, we each have a measure of courage but can find ourselves shrinking back at the last second.

Fear of failure locks us into a pattern of making promises we don't honor.

We need to think of uncomfortable moments as character developers in disguise. We can always choose to put our best foot forward no matter the circumstances. Easier said than done, I realize. My voice teacher told me many years ago that integrity begins with small things. She said that if I was faithful to keep the promises I made to myself, I could be trusted to keep the promises I made to others. The scriptures say it this way: "He who is faithful in a very little thing is faithful also in much; and he who is unrighteous in a very little thing is unrighteous also in much" (Luke 6:10 NASB).

At the Naval Academy, midshipmen appear to be risk averse since the culture encourages success and excellence. Within the Gospel Choir, however, students seemed willing to try uncomfortable things, like singing a solo in front of everyone. The culture of the Gospel Choir provides support and encouragement for all its members.

I always smile when I think of audition season at the Academy. Incoming plebes come to the Academy for six weeks prior to the start of the school term in August. That month and a half is called Plebe Summer and serves as a boot camp designed to indoctrinate each new student in naval culture, verbal responses to authority, expectations, regulations, uniform codes, and more. All civilian personal effects are taken from them—watches, cell phones, clothing, etc. Women cannot wear their hair past collar-length, while men receive a crew cut.

During this intense adjustment period students can participate in chapel choir each week, and at the end of plebe summer they can audition for the choir they'd like to join for the school year. Since music is such a great stress reliever, many students who cannot sing attend auditions. After several weeks of plebe summer, they will do anything to escape the detailers. They know they can't sing. I know they can't sing. Random folks walking by the audition room know it too.

To add insult to injury, by the time auditions occur, many midshipmen are suffering from something called "plebe hack." The hack is a severe case of hoarseness resulting from weeks of constant yelling, sometimes combined with a respiratory infection.

In front of the other plebes, these young leaders face their fears and sing, shout, or sometimes wheeze their way through an audition with the gusto of a determined asthmatic. Over the years I learned to control my facial expressions no matter what. I even developed a simple phrase for poor singers: "I hear a singing heart, but I don't believe I hear a singing voice."

Life presents us with opportunities to face our fears. This may mean confronting friends or family, speaking out against injustice or confessing our wrongdoing and facing the consequences.

Standing in front of others can make us feel exposed and inadequate even when we know how important the opportunity is. It can be tempting to look for a way to escape, but a decade with midshipmen taught me a simple template for sidestepping fear to act in faith: "Ask, Trust, Try."

During a regular choir rehearsal in the fall of 2012, I needed a soloist for William McDowell's "I Belong to You." I opened the floor for those who wanted to try out, but no one budged. Instantly in my spirit I heard the name of one of the tenors, whom I'll call Adam Sanchez. I asked him to come down from the risers and try the solo. He looked surprised but did as I asked. As he began singing, the choir encouraged him. Not only did he have a compelling voice, but also we could sense the presence of God as he sang. When he finished, the choir exploded in applause.

After rehearsal, I received this note from Adam:

Hey, Ms. Scott,

I was trying to talk to you after rehearsal. I just wanted to tell you about a conversation I had just last night with my girlfriend. She asked if I was still going to be on Gospel Choir next year. I told her of course, and she replied, "Good. Because I want you to get a solo next year." I laughed and said that the only way that was going to happen was if God gave me the courage to audition or if you chose me yourself. Sure enough, the very next evening, you called me out. Then the very next song we sang was "God has spoken, let the church say amen." I just could not get over the message that God was sending me in that. He made me realize that even when I don't believe in myself, He does.

I was nervous when I was singing but that's something that will fade with time. I know that God's plan for me is more than just getting over my stage fright. I really want to perform this solo and would be honored. Thank you for calling me out and revealing God's path for me. God bless.

Several scriptures flood my mind when I think of Adam's experience, but none is more fitting than Isaiah 65:24 (NASB): "It will also come to pass that before they call, I will answer; and while they are still speaking, I will hear." Not only did the Lord assure Adam that his prayers were received and important, but God's answer gave him the courage to step past fear and try something new.

Ask

Asking refers to prayer. It is important to seek God before an opportunity presents itself. Proverbs 3:5-6 (NKJV) says, "Trust in the LORD with all your heart, and lean not on your understanding; in all your ways acknowledge Him, and He shall direct your paths."

Many times opportunities come our way, and we say "No" without seeking God's will. How often have we missed a wonderful blessing because it did not come packaged in a way that appealed to us? Often as leaders we have a clear idea of the type of spouse, organization, culture, brand, or ministry we want to be involved with, but no one knows what we need better than God.

I fell victim to substituting my desires for the Lord's plans more than once as it related to choir membership. On two occasions midshipmen auditioned for me and they could not sing at all. In one case a student auditioned for me three years in a row and was never selected. During their senior year my Officer Representative encouraged me to let the student into the choir. I refused and gave the officer my reasons. That night, however, I went home and asked the Lord. To my surprise I had a clear release in my spirit to invite the student with no singing ability into the choir. They joined us for one year and brought such tremendous joy, focus, and strong work ethic that it transformed the section in which they "sang."

In the second case a singer had a weak ear, but when I prayed and invited them to join, I gained a faithful intercessor whose willingness to fast and pray made a difference in the seamless execution of our tours. Although these students were not great singers, the Lord used them in ways that furthered his purposes for the Gospel Choir.

Trust

After asking God to show us his will, we have to trust his answer. The King James Bible dictionary defines *trust* as "confidence; a reliance or resting of the mind on the integrity, veracity, justice, friendship or other sound principle of another person."[27] Jeremiah 17:7-8 echoes that idea:

27 "Trust," KingJamesBibleDictionary.com, accessed Sept. 13, 2017, http://kingjamesbibledictionary.com/Dictionary/trust.

But blessed is the man who trusts me, GOD, the woman who sticks with GOD. They are like trees replanted in Eden, putting down roots near the rivers—never a worry through the hottest of summers, never dropping a leaf, serene and calm through droughts, bearing fresh fruit every season. (MSG)

When we trust God, he will supply everything we need to be strong from the inside out. He will teach us how to strengthen our people, infrastructure, systems, and teams to withstand hardship without sacrificing productivity.

When I trusted God by adding non-singers to the choir, he honored his Word by making us productive and strong in areas where we had not been in the past.

Try

Finally we need to step out, obey the Lord, and do the new thing, knowing that he will honor our obedience. When Adam stepped forward to sing that night, God honored him by bringing an immediate blessing to all of us who heard him.

The added benefit of faith is that our obedience influences others. In other words, when we follow Christ, we can expect others to follow us. Toward the end of 1 Corinthians, the apostle Paul revealed four keys:

Live a life that is a blessing and not an offense.

Live a life worthy of imitation.

Make Jesus the pattern in all decision making.

Follow other leaders as they follow Christ. (In short, faith is contagious.)

After my student Adam's success with the solo in our choir, a few other tenors tried out for the same solo. I am convinced that they were encouraged by his act of boldness.

A Good Template

One of my hobbies is design. I love arranging colors, shapes, and objects in a way that is attractive and inviting. Over the years I've taken note of the elements I like best. These recurring ideas are a template of sorts. For example, in my homes I've enjoyed neutrals accented with bright colors, graphic black-and-white patterns, and metallic objects.

The Word of God is filled with what I like to call "faith templates." These are stories of how other believers acted in faith and pleased God. We can pray and apply those principles to our own lives.

"Ask, Trust, Try" is one of God's faith templates, but scripture contains many other templates for acting in faith. Two come to mind:

Queen Esther used a "fasting + boldness" template to overcome her fear of approaching the king so that her people, the Jews, would be saved from extermination.

Jesus used the "prayer + self-denial" template in the Garden of Gethsemane to overcome his desire to turn back from going to the cross.

I encourage you to study the scripture for other examples of acting in faith instead of fear. As an influencer, the people who follow you depend on you and your willingness to be an example of one who walks in faith.

CHAPTER TEN

EMBRACE NOW, RECALL WHEN

THE POWER OF PERSPECTIVE

"The only thing that is constant is change."
—Heraclitus

When the Lord led me away from pursuing an operatic career and pointed my life in the direction of church work and teaching, I endured several years where listening to young classical singers perform made me sad and resentful. For a long time I wished to be in their shoes, and it hurt that I wasn't. I knew I was obeying God, but that didn't make my desires disappear overnight. I had trained for many years to become a classical singer. I showed the talent, promise, and focus it took to have an international career. Walking away from something I loved that much was excruciating and difficult to explain to the many people who had supported me over the years. I share this because I think it's important to be honest. Too often believers talk about the results of obeying God but not the frustration of doing so.

I slowly accepted the idea that the Lord was asking me to support others and push them into their season of greatness while denying myself. I mentally packed away my dreams and focused on the singing I was able to do. I must confess: at first I obeyed hoping that the Lord would see me, take pity and let me go back to opera. I soon learned that the Lord never asks us to give something up without giving us something in exchange. God asked me to leave classical music, and when I did, he gave me a genuine passion for his presence. I began to lead worship regularly and write worship music, but more importantly I began to spend hours alone with him. Once I got to know the Lord intimately, classical music became something I sang infrequently and my desire to be a classical singer eventually disappeared.

During a women's conference in 2006, one of the pastors pointed me out and declared that the Lord had placed a crown on my head and was bringing me to the forefront. She went on to say that the Lord would reopen closed musical doors.

Another prophetic word from South African Pastor Jerome Liberty came in 2010. In it God urged me to get up and move. He told me that I was standing in a place that was too small for the vision he had for my life.

In December 2009, I went to a wedding in Nassau, Bahamas. The guest who sat next to me at the reception was a college professor. As we talked, he told me that going back to school to earn a doctorate would open doors for me. As he spoke, something ignited in my heart, but I didn't want to go back to school. At that point I felt like I had been either enrolled in or teaching at a school my entire life, and I wouldn't hear of it.

Little did I know his suggestion would be the key that activated both prophetic words I'd received. After praying about the professor's advice, I applied to my alma mater, the University of Maryland at College Park. I am ashamed to say that I didn't submit my application until after the deadline had passed, hoping that a late submission would disqualify me. I was in a state of disobedience. After a series of unlikely events, the School of Music accepted me and, to my surprise, offered me a full scholarship in the form of a teaching assistantship. My days were soon filled with teaching undergraduate music courses and voice lessons, taking graduate courses, and preparing for performances. I was blessed to complete that degree in 2016.

After more than a decade away from opera, my voice was still in fine shape and responded well to intense training, but it felt surreal to sing music I had given up for so long. I kept searching my heart for the thirst for fame I'd once had, but it simply wasn't there. I enjoyed singing, and audiences seemed to enjoy hearing me, but the desire to become a world-famous opera singer no longer consumed me.

Halfway through my degree program, I had the opportunity to sing on a masterclass for the world-renowned soprano, Frederica von Stade, who had many kind things to say about my performance. She has since become a generous advocate and encourager. After singing for her, I couldn't help but reflect on the years when I'd struggled to let go of my classical dreams. A version of my dreams had died, but God's plan to use my voice for his glory never did. I have yet to experience all he has for me as a singer, classical or otherwise. As Paul wrote: "There has never been the slightest doubt in my mind that the God who started this great work in [me] would keep at it and bring it to a flourishing finish on the very day Christ Jesus appears" (Phil. 1:6 MSG).

After watching my classical dreams seemingly fall to the ground and die, only to be brought back to life by the Lord, I can't help but draw a parallel to my later work at the Academy. There, I worked to plant the seed of God's Word in the hearts of midshipmen with the expectation that the Lord would cause those seeds to spring up at the right time. I prayed that the words of our choir songs would provide comfort, encouragement, and strength after graduation, through deployments, long days at sea, training, relocations, and more. I also prayed that they would bring forth a harvest in each life where they would be planted.

When that growth process would begin in someone's life, I often received messages like this one

STEADY FAITH • 125

from a former student I'll call Ensign Patterson, who sent a letter to the choir the fall after graduation:

I hope that my message finds you all well and encouraged. Currently, I am deployed and let's just say life isn't so easy. I can't stress it enough, take advantage of the time you have now. Often, and I did it too, we blow off school or classes thinking, "Oh I will do it tomorrow." Well, tomorrow can easily turn into years. It is a cliché we all have heard many times, but it starts now. Learn all that you can about the community you want to join. Ask questions, and when you think you don't have any more to ask, ask someone, "What questions should I be asking?"

I have had my highs and my very lows when I have been out here, but God has kept me above it all. Because I believe, trust, and have faith, I rise above what the devil tries to lay before me to block my path.

There is no choir out here and more often than not it is just you, God, and the Bible. Cherish the time you have with each other. Prepare yourselves for battle. I love you all and miss you more than you know. You are loved, and you are blessed. Be encouraged.

At the time of this writing, Patterson is a first lieutenant in the surface warfare community—or in layman's terms, an officer who drives warships. Shore duty brought Lt. Patterson back to the Naval

Academy after several years on deployment. As we spoke recently, I could see glimpses of that young midshipman from the past, especially during humorous moments, yet the authoritative bearing of a seasoned officer was unmistakable. Over the years, this lieutenant has learned to address military and spiritual matters with command presence and wisdom. What a tremendous testimony this officer's life has become to the Academy and the Lord.

Thanks to social media I can keep up with a decade of choir members on various platforms. I have watched many get married, become parents, and of course serve our nation in locations around the world. As their careers advance, they reveal less about themselves on social media—wisely so. Still, it is always a pleasure to connect in person or online. Like clockwork, sometime in the first two years following graduation, I received letters that expressed great memories of the choir and feelings of nostalgia. This series of letters is representative of that sentiment:

Ms. Scott,

I hope you are doing extremely well and just wanted to say how much I truly appreciated the encouragement you've always blessed me with while in GC. It's very different being thrust into the world from our very loving Gospel Choir environment, and not gonna lie, I really miss the Gospel Choir. I have definitely been blessed with your encouragement in faith, which has helped me with a lot of my training and just wanted to thank you. I pray that you continue to refresh the hearts of those around you and please keep me in your prayers as I continue prepare for my job.

Hi Ms. Scott,

I've been following the choir online the past few months and it looks like y'all are doing big things and having a great time. I think about the choir all the time. So many great memories from those short four years by the Bay came from my time with the Choir. Joining the choir during Plebe Summer was one of the best decisions I have made. Being able to able to travel and represent our Lord and the Academy was a very humbling and rewarding experience.

I am certain that when other classes begin to depart Annapolis they too will look back and recall how special the United States Naval Academy Gospel Choir was to them as well.

Hey Ms. Scott!

I just wanted to reach out to you and talk to you about a fulfillment of a word of prophecy you gave me back my plebe year.

I'm not sure if you remember, but it was during a time after a rehearsal where were just letting the Holy Spirit act. You called me to the front with you and you told me that God had a special woman in mind for me and not to try to force it to happen with the different girls that will be in my life, but be patient. Well I can't say that I stayed clear of my share of heartbreak but I just wanted to let you know that I did find that woman God prepared for me and I'm marrying her tomorrow!

Hey Ms. Scott:
I just wanted to shoot you a message to tell you that I'm thinking about you. In conversations where new contacts question me about the Naval Academy, I often discuss the role of GC in the support community I found at USNA. I know that you must feel the impact you have on all of us, but I wanted to explicitly thank you for the countless memories I created with GC and the strength of faith I felt through the music. While I remain somewhat sad that I will never find a group that rivals the specialness of GC, I am so much more grateful for the experiences I had because of that uniqueness.

As promised, I am going to look for volunteer opportunities this summer. Thank you again for being a tremendous role model in faith and kindness!

As officers go out on deployment after deployment, receive promotions, and become a bit more seasoned, the letters they've written have reflected greater maturity and the distinct changes in perspective that growth brings. This is when the seeds have become plants and are beginning to bear fruit.

Graduates who've served in the fleet for three or more years write with urgency and a sober viewpoint. As in the letters below, they often admonish current choir members to treasure the guidance, connection to God, and spiritual impartation available in Gospel Choir. With the benefit of time and distance, they are able to see the long-term blessings gained from the choir. So many officers write to say that the Gospel Choir songs are still rising out of their hearts to encourage them many years later. Whenever I've received a letter like that, it would strengthen my resolve to keep introducing songs based on scripture. And so I remained determined to teach the Word in song because I understood the impact it would have for years to come.

Hey Ms. Scott!

You, the band and GC have been on my heart lately. Going through some of the toughest training in my life mentally, physically and spiritually! Please tell the choir that I love them and to please, please, please HIDE THE WORD OF GOD IN THEIR HEARTS! If they get anything out of being in GC, hold on to a song and the scripture contained in it. Doing that has gotten me through my darkest days here.

Please remind them to cherish the environment they're in—I know it's hard to as a mid but God has placed a foundation there like no other place I have been in my entire military career. Please tell them to take FULL advantage of it and to get all the understanding and wisdom He has available at USNA.

Miss Scott,

I truly miss both you and the choir. You have done such a great job leading the choir both musically and spiritually. The Lord has handpicked you to lead the choir for a specific reason: so that He can perform great works through you that affect the choir and those that have a chance to hear the choir sing. God has chosen you to be the director of the Gospel Choir because he knows that you have a strong faith, one that turns to the Lord for guidance. It is for this reason that you are able to bring the light of the Lord to others in dark times. The choir has grown closer together through faith and there is no doubt in my mind that it is the work of God through you. An amazing gift has been given to you, the gift and opportunity to effectively support and lift the faith of others. To whom much is given, much is demanded. I am blessed to have you be a part of my life and I wish you the very best in the future. God loves you and so do I.

Ms. Scott!

I was thinking about you. Just wanted to tell you I love and miss you! I know you're on tour and I pray that God is moving like never before.

The military is changing as a whole. It's easy to see when you're in a training pipeline like flight school, since you have a huge mix of new officers, and people who have been doing this for ten years and twenty. As this change takes place we continually need officers of right moral standing, sound judgment, and a sense of the Holy Spirit working in their lives. I believe that's what you are preparing in Gospel Choir. When you are on your own, you are really on your own here. Gospel Choir almost acts as a conduit for midshipmen. You really need to want a relationship and fellowship with believers to find a group even remotely similar to Gospel Choir.

God does things so well. Let me tell you with tears in my eyes, if it had not been for the Lord on my side I can only imagine where I would be. It is amazing what God has done.

These letters are among the many treasures I received as I served this community of leaders. Like jewels in a crown, they are evidence of God at work long after officers leave the Academy—showing the power of perspective.

CHAPTER ELEVEN

FOLLOW THE LEADER

THE POWER OF MENTORS

Mentors have guided me during every season of my life. My first mentor was my mother. Although her given name was Marye Lucille, many knew her as "Aunt Marye." Tall, brown, and slender, she was incredibly brilliant and beautiful. We lived in a wonderfully decorated home usually filled with good food, family, friends, and neighborhood kids she easily took under her wing. She worked outside the home as a teacher and remained God-fearing, funny, and generous. To this day I don't understand how she did it all. I don't mean to suggest that my mother was perfect, because she had her flaws just like anyone else. She could be hot-tempered and extremely blunt, and could stop you in your tracks with just a look. I lived with my mother day in and day out for eighteen years until I left for college, and like most daughters I observed her carefully. I noted her strengths and weaknesses, her brilliance and challenges. She made a practice of serving others with her life. From providing a meal to opening our home when extended family and friends needed a place to stay, she always found a way to help. From her I learned that serving others is a powerful way to lead.

Serving others is a powerful way to lead.

While all leaders come under the scrutiny of others, servant leaders welcome this observation. They are transparent. Their lives seem to say: "Stand close and watch as I lead. See how I recover from mishaps and notice how I negotiate power."

I've been blessed to know many servant-leaders over the years, and some of the finest have been the military members and Officer Reps I worked with at the Academy. They did whatever was required to oversee and guide our midshipmen.

Good Oversight, Good Leader

At the Naval Academy every midshipman club or extracurricular activity requires an Officer Representative (O-Rep). O-Reps make sure that students are meeting the protocol standards, procedures, and regulations required by the Naval Academy.

Gospel Choir O-Reps introduce themselves to the choir bristling with military bearing, perfect uniforms, command presence, and words of wisdom. Midshipmen admire these characteristics and aspire to display them, but officers who make the greatest impact are also approachable and transparent. Young leaders are desperate to see someone model protocol standards balanced with human transparency.

O-Reps perform more tasks than I could name, but I'd like to focus on three functions: oversight, mentorship, and serving as a future resource for young officers.

Oversight: Kennedy Center Honors

In the winter of 2014, the Gospel Choir was asked to perform at the Kennedy Center Honors as part of the military tribute to actor Tom Hanks. Each year the Honors are rehearsed and recorded in secret so that the honorees have no idea what performers to expect. Our choir members learned the music before the Thanksgiving holiday, then we rehearsed and taped the show at the Kennedy Center for two days in December.

The first day of rehearsals went smoothly. We learned the onstage blocking, which is a bit like choreography, then we prerecorded the vocal performance.

We returned the next day for the live show. We were asked to arrive at 10:00 a.m., but the program would not begin until 8:00 p.m. that night. In the interim we rehearsed again, and the midshipmen studied, ate, slept, and played games to pass the time. There was also a brief window of time when the midshipmen were able to meet a few celebrities they admired, such as R&B singers Usher and Bruno Mars. They also met the a cappella group Pentatonix.

In addition to the honorees, celebrity audience members, and performers, President and First Lady Obama would be in attendance, so security was exceptionally tight. Even though the midshipmen were in uniform, there were several screening checkpoints and secure holding rooms, each manned by military police or Secret Service. There was never a time during the performance day that we were not under the watchful eye of security personnel.

Military security and Secret Service functioned like a well-oiled machine. They stayed in constant contact with one another and made sure we were always in the right place at the right time. Although they were cordial, they were not jovial or overly friendly with us. When small details caught their attention, the air of authority they carried became heightened. No one had to tell us to keep our voices down or to remain respectful. The presence and demeanor of the security team demanded it. I tell this story because it reminds me of the eagle-eyed oversight of Officer Representatives and the weight their authority carries with the midshipmen at the Academy.

Mentorship: Lighthouses and Midwives

When I think of the mentoring roles of an O-Rep, lighthouses and midwives come to mind. Lighthouses guide sea vessels to safety, away from dangerous coastlines. They tower over rocky, solitary places while emitting such an intense light that the difference between dangerous ground and safe water becomes evident. It's easy to see the parallels to real leadership in that description. Mature leaders should serve as a beacon to young, inexperienced leaders. Officer Reps are "lighthouse leaders" whose wisdom guides midshipmen toward safe courses of action while teaching them to avoid delays and unnecessary pitfalls.

During the writing of this book, I visited the newly opened National Museum of African American Art and Culture located on the National Mall in Washington, DC. While there, I saw a short film about the role midwives played in the African American community from Reconstruction until the mid 1970s. In the film African American midwives were seen delivering, cleaning, and weighing newborns. These women worked quickly and didn't seem the least bit timid, even when handling tiny babies. They knew the secret: newborns are stronger than they appear. That knowledge informed the confident way the midwives moved.

This observation reminded me of Officer Reps at the Academy. Like midwives O-Reps ensure the safe completion of each mission while preventing minor issues from becoming major ones. In the case of the Gospel Choir, the term *mission* referred to every performance or tour we undertook. Midshipmen leaders were responsible for planning, executing, and communicating every detail, from transportation and logistics to attendance and equipment needs. With such a large touring group, we always had glitches and mistakes that led to a reprimand. In the early years I'd cringe inside when student leaders found themselves on the receiving end of an O-Rep's blunt displeasure. Over the years I came to see the wisdom in their rebuke. Like midwives O-Reps knew that midshipmen were more resilient than they thought they were, especially in the face of uncomfortable correction.

Resource: Securing the Future

My friend Dr. Lester Green is a gifted musician and fellow alum of the University of Maryland. For the fifteen years that we've known each other, he's been a tremendous resource for me. Although it is not something I've ever sought out, he's informed me of job openings, asked me to perform at high-profile events, and recommended me for great musical opportunities. Not only does his assistance speak volumes about his respect for my musical gifts, but also it's a testament of his unselfishness. I am grateful for his support.

Similarly Officer Reps often become a resource for young officers as they start their military careers. In many cases the mentoring relationships formed at the Academy between students and O-Reps prove invaluable over the entire course of that young officer's career.

Raising the Standard of Excellence

Ultimately by providing oversight, mentoring, and acting as a resource, Officer Reps change the organizations they serve for the better. I served alongside at least twenty Reps, and each of them helped to raise the standard of excellence within the choir.

When I first began directing the Gospel Choir, it was hard to tell whether I worked for the Officer Reps, or if they worked for me. I subsequently discovered that things weren't quite that clear cut. Depending upon the task, we deferred to one another.

The personalities of our O-Reps ran the gamut from scholarly to serious, from introspective to humorous. The common threads I observed were an unwavering love for our country, respect for their rank and its responsibilities, pride in the young leaders in the Gospel Choir, and a strong desire to keep us on course.

Most officers displayed a professional, no-nonsense demeanor at the beginning of the year. As choir tours got underway, however, O-Reps showed more of their personality to the midshipmen. One O-Rep used to prepare words of wisdom (riddled with puns) and deliver them to us on the bus as we traveled from venue to venue. Another would join us onstage and sing our final song. By the end of the first tour, they were often singing along during our concerts, doing the choreography (when no one was looking, of course), taking photos like proud parents, and congratulating the choir on their performances.

By displaying their humanity O-Reps showed the mids how to strike a balance between military bearing and transparency. O-Reps could be stern yet show compassion. One response did not negate the other. This too taught midshipmen the balance of good leadership.

Military Accomplishments

One Rep worked tirelessly to raise the academic standards required for participation in the choir. When that officer left, the scholarly culture of the choir was completely transformed and has remained high until the time of this writing.

Two Officer Reps worked tirelessly to increase our national visibility, and under their leadership the Gospel Choir joined the Glee Clubs to perform at the 2009 Inaugural Concert for President Barack Obama on the steps of the Lincoln Memorial. During that performance we served as the backing choir for soprano Rene Fleming, pop artist Beyoncé Knowles, and other musical acts. As a result of the efforts of our Officer Reps, we also performed the national anthem for both NFL and NBA teams while touring the country.

Officer Reps didn't just impact the midshipmen; they also informed my leadership style and taught me how to ensure the choir's longevity by making sure it added value at the Academy.

As a result, when I served alongside younger, less experienced O-Reps, I was able to pay that knowledge forward. The scriptures tell us in Proverbs 27:17 that "iron sharpens iron." In matters of leadership development, this sentiment is also a foundational truth, because all of us need mentors in our lives if we are to become all that God has in mind for us.

CHAPTER TWELVE

WILDERNESS AND OASIS

THE POWER OF JOURNEY

We couldn't see them, but we could hear them. As all fifty Gospel Choir members and our band exited the tour bus and began to walk through the campus of the Soong Eui Girls' High School, the volume increased. The sound came from several hundred girls screaming and cheering for us from the open windows of classroom buildings and dormitories. I glanced behind me to see midshipmen grinning in shock at this over-the-top greeting. For a split second I'm sure they felt like rock stars. Our goodwill tour to Seoul, South Korea, in the spring of 2011 had just become very exciting.

Overwhelmed by Appreciation

By the time we entered the school's auditorium, our musical gear was in place thanks to the efforts of a local crew hired to support our tour. Theatre-style seats secured to a wooden floor filled the brightly lit room. A small wooden stage, raised about five feet above the ground, accommodated our choir and four-piece band with little room to spare. After sound-check, the school's young women began to file in until there were nearly a thousand students plus their teachers. Dressed in the standard sweater, blouse, and plaid skirt that would have identified them as students anywhere in the world, our audience was friendly and energetic, and greeted us warmly.

The choir sang the songs we'd prepared with even more energy than normal as they fed off the girls' energy and excitement. If you've ever seen old video footage of musical concerts filled with high-pitched screams, the reactions at Soong Eui were pretty similar.

To end our concerts, we'd teach the audience a simple dance and chorus. It was a way to engage listeners, particularly at high schools, and it also gave everyone a chance to move around after listening for an hour. We did the interactive number at Soong Eui High School, but there was no way we could have predicted what happened next.

Students ran to the stage, then hoisted one another up until the choir and band were hemmed in by at least fifty girls, and they just kept coming. As school officials intervened, the girls left the stage and continued dancing on the floor. I can honestly say that I've never seen a more excited or appreciative audience anywhere in the world.

As you might imagine, that concert was the musical highlight of the tour. When we left Seoul and traveled to the three other cities on our tour—Busan, Daegu, and Chinhae (home of the Republic of Korea Naval Academy)—each new audience was appreciative and gave us standing ovations. We sang at various universities, churches, and high schools. If Soong Eui Girls' school was the most exciting visit, the most meaningful visit was to the Korean Naval Academy, where our students met and interacted with their Korean shipmates.

Meeting Counterparts

Our American midshipmen stayed overnight in the dorms at the Republic of Korea Naval Academy. Paired with Korean mids who shared the same rank, class, and leadership role, they got the chance to meet and interact with true counterparts. Though separated by language and culture, the common threads of service to one's country, leadership training, and life at a naval military academy seemed to help students from both countries form quick friendships. I suspect that many of those friendships are intact today, as students from two cultures have now become officers in both navies.

Showcasing America, Respecting Korea

Our mission to South Korea had several objectives. First, our concerts provided Korean audiences (both civilian and military) a glimpse into American culture. In the case of the Gospel Choir, Koreans came away with an ethnically diverse snapshot of America and of military members who are free to express a common faith. Second, many of the midshipmen got a chance to represent the United States as international ambassadors. Finally, through briefings by American officers stationed in Seoul and meetings with Korean navy and Marine Corps officers, our students got to see how other nations perceive the American military. Many of our students, dressed in civilian clothing, toured the DMZ (demilitarized zone) on the border of North and South Korea. Standing only steps away from a nation crushed by totalitarian rule served as a sobering reminder of the freedoms we have in the United States.

In the spirit of Steven Covey's famous concept "Seek first to understand, then to be understood," our midshipmen started each concert with the Korean national anthem sung in the native language. This demonstration of respect resonated with our audiences, as evidenced by their warm and prolonged applause. I am profoundly grateful to have taken part in a tour that showed America's diversity to a culture halfway around the world.

Appreciation and Excellence

Another important leadership takeaway occurred to me after I had time to process the overwhelming reception at Soong Eui Girls' High School—one that bothered me at first.

For years the Gospel Choir performed all over the United States for truly appreciative audiences. Still, our most appreciative American audiences were no match for the enthusiastic girls in Seoul. If I'm honest, for a few days after that performance, I compared Americans and Koreans—and judged Americans harshly. I wondered why our fellow citizens didn't respond with the joy the Korean girls displayed. As time has passed, I realized that by playing the "Which audience appreciated us more?" game, I was missing the two leadership lessons the Lord was trying to teach me: First, leaders must do their jobs with excellence whether encouragement is abundant or scarce; and second, honor plays a strategic role in leadership development.

The Leadership Journey

Writers and speakers often describe life as a journey, a marathon, or some other arduous process. These metaphors are accurate; however, the life of a leader requires more. If life is a marathon, leadership is like running that marathon through a wilderness. I use the word *wilderness* because it suggests a place of overgrown vegetation with no visible pathway. In other words leaders run the marathon of life through uncharted territory under the watchful eyes of those that follow them. Leaders must take responsibility for the safety of those they serve.

Learning to lead isn't about receiving accolades; it's about serving others and staying the course as they follow your lead. Growing as a leader will require you to give the best of yourself whether your team receives you with polite restraint or overwhelming acclaim. Leadership is about facing and overcoming challenges. It is not a path for the faint of heart.

Challenge vs. Honor

Now, before I leave you with a single-sided view of leadership—one that only discusses its challenges—I'd like you to reconsider the Korean girls' school. Our choir responded so positively to their overwhelming appreciation for one simple reason: those young women honored us. Their display of gratitude refreshed us. When it comes to leadership development, challenges help us to grow, but being honored encourages us to continue

Challenges help us to grow; honor encourages us to continue.

We all remember elementary school science class where we learned that if a chunk of carbon undergoes intense pressure and heat long enough, a diamond can form. By the time I was in college, this scientific process had also become a metaphor of encouragement, reminding me that persevering through tough times would ultimately yield good things.

I still believe that pressure and challenges are two of the greatest tools for producing solid leaders. At first leadership development can seem like a never-ending test of one's endurance. Though it's uncomfortable, submission to the process strips away the immature and unproductive aspects of our character, revealing a more focused, streamlined version of ourselves. God can do more with what's left than he could have with the baggage we once carried. For this reason leadership development is never easy, whether through some formal program like the Naval Academy, or the life lessons orchestrated by God. Training will either be effective or easy—never both.

The Frequent Oasis

Unlike the nonstop pressure required to transform carbon into a gemstone, the Lord sends strategic moments of relief during our leadership development journey, because rest and encouragement are beneficial to us in the long run. For this truth I am grateful! Brief moments of relief and reward function like an oasis. The reaction of the audience at the girls' school was such a moment for the Gospel Choir.

During the school year Gospel Choir rehearsals also serve as an oasis for midshipmen. The uplifting music and sense of family encourage young leaders and provide the chance to decompress after a week of nonstop requirements. After meetings each midshipman is inspired to get back to the task at hand.

The Benchmark Oasis

The year 2017 marked my tenth as Gospel Choir director at the Naval Academy. At our annual Black History Month concert in February, I was surprised to see so many choir alumni in the audience. Their presence raised my spirits because I knew we'd be saying farewell to our current O-Rep, who'd once been a member of the gospel choir. It was so rewarding to have that officer return to serve the choir, but new orders meant a new duty station. The choir sang an upbeat, inspired performance, and when it ended, I prepared myself to say good-bye to our Rep.

When she stepped to the podium, she confessed that she wasn't there to say good-bye. Instead she was there to honor me for ten years of service to the Naval Academy. The alumni and current choir members, my band, and even my boss were all in on the surprise. That night I received flowers and kind words from current and former students, and then in the most significant gesture of respect, ten individuals gave me shoulder boards. Shoulder boards display the rank or level of authority of the military member wearing them. From the lowliest plebe midshipman up to a First Lieutenant currently on active duty, I received a tangible representation of my ten years of service to them. By handing me their "authority," each student or officer was saying "Thank you" for the part I'd played in their success.

It never occurred to me that I'd be honored that evening. After ten years of service, my thoughts were always on covering the midshipmen in prayer, meeting the needs of the choir, managing the band, being a team player in the music department, and bringing glory to God through it all.

The Performance Oasis

As I was writing this chapter, I called my voice teacher, Carmen Balthrop, who has been in my life so long that her family has become my family. She is a mentor, wise counselor, and trusted confidant. She is also a world-class operatic soprano with countless premieres, performances around the world, recordings, awards, and honors to her credit. As a performer she serves people by sharing her musical talent with them, so I wanted to get her take on audience response. I wanted to know if she perceived polite audiences differently than over-the-top ones, and if she had a preference for either. Did it hurt her feelings when listeners didn't seem wildly enthusiastic? Did it make her feel like she was a better performer when she received a loud, standing ovation?

Her response was completely unexpected.

She told me that when she prepares for performances, she doesn't factor in audience response at all. I was shocked. Didn't she care if they liked her performance? Didn't she hear the roar of the crowd in her head? Don't all performers, especially opera divas, have egos? I needed to hear more.

She went on to explain that performance is an opportunity to communicate something, not to stroke her ego. Whether the audience reacts to her music with applause, shouts, and cheers, or with quiet appreciation, the most important thing is resonance. In other words, did her musical performance echo something the audience already believes? Did she repeat a sentiment her audience values? When the answer is "Yes," an audience will respond positively—every time. Many years ago she told me that compliments were like perfume: pleasant if sniffed, harmful if swallowed. In other words, Leader, your reason for leading, influencing, and serving others must be motivated by something other than self-gratification. Her "others first" approach to performance reveals maturity and wisdom, and creates the kind of oasis that refreshes performer and audience simultaneously.

So far we've seen the power of the frequent oasis, the benchmark oasis, and the performance oasis. Our final example is the most powerful of all.

The Continual Oasis

What do you do when none of the external oasis types are providing the encouragement you need? In those moments you must turn to the continual oasis.

I didn't come up with this concept. In fact I am borrowing it from our favorite, King David.

I've mentioned that David was a warrior, king, and prophet throughout this book. Not only was he a gifted musician and songwriter, but his life was full of glorious and tragic moments making him a perfect example of what to do and what *not* to do. One of his greatest strengths was his ability to encourage himself in the Lord. Many of his songs as found in the book Psalms followed a familiar pattern.

First he would pour out his heart to God about his enemies, false friends, fatigue, fear, and more. Immediately after complaining, David would begin to talk about the greatness of God. Finally he would remind himself of the times God gave him the strategies to overcome obstacles, or he would rehearse the victories God had given him in battle. Next David would focus on God's attributes: his faithfulness, mercy, authority, and loving-kindness.

By the end of most of his psalms, David had created an oasis by giving praise to God. By taking the time to remember how trustworthy and powerful God was, David's faith increased and his fears vanished. Psalm 22 follows this pattern. Verses 1-18 list David's complaints and fears. In verses 19-26 he remembers God's goodness. And throughout verses 19-31 David offers praise to God in his current circumstances and for his future.

This strategy still works today. As I was in the midst of finishing this book, I knew I needed to follow David's strategy, because the Lord was asking me to take the next step in my own journey of faith—and after a decade, to bid a fond farewell to the Naval Academy. He allowed me the time I needed to adjust and prepare. I departed with a strong sense of God's peace and a tremendous excitement about what comes next.

So follow David's example, share your burdens with God—but don't stop there. Look back and remember how he has already led you to overcome hard times, challenges, and trials. You're here today on your journey because the Lord orchestrated circumstances to help you through. If he did it once, he will do so again. Praise and thank God for the outcome you desire, then put your faith in action for the journey ahead!

Conclusion

L eader, influencer – or however you think of yourself - please know that there are many tools (both tangible and spiritual) to assist you on your journey of service to others. Trust that the challenges you face today are building your tomorrow. Know that moments of honor will come to refresh you. Remember to keep an "others first" mind-set in service, and remain strengthened by drinking from the continual oasis. Above all know that strength from God is available to you to meet every assignment and accomplish every task.

I pray that good success will be yours as you lead, serve, and influence others. May those you impact in your workplace or ministry, industry or home, be forever blessed because they encountered your faith, compassion, correction, and guidance. May you always display steady faith!

Acknowledgements

Gina Adams, thank you for suggesting that I reach beyond my academic research and include personal and spiritual elements in this work. You are God's mouthpiece.

Dr. Michael Williams, yours was the voice of reason I counted on to bring focus and clarity to the early draft. As both a retired Marine Corps officer and an academic, your perspective is rare, yet exactly what I needed to think critically about this manuscript. Thanks for your time, valued opinion, and trusted red pen!

Stacey Evans Morgan, dear friend, sister and trusted confidant, I appreciate your ability to inhabit the space of writer and reader with equal facility. Thanks for your unfailing encouragement, leading questions, humor and eagle-eyed edits!

To my editor, John David Kudrick, you're absolutely amazing – kind but firm, quick to respond and always filled with Godly encouragement. You polished the manuscript, educated me and cut away the unnecessary fluff with such incredible grace. The Lord has truly anointed you for the work you do. Thank you!

Carmen, Patrick, Camille, Aaron, Micah and Verna, thank you for allowing me to work on this project for months while being less present than usual in each of your lives. Just try and get rid of me now. Ha!

Gina, thanks for the vibrant cover. Derrel Todd, thank you for your joyful spirit and for so many amazing images, it was hard to choose just one. Shauné Hayes, thank for your incredible makeup artistry and kind spirit.

To the incredible women of influence whose words of endorsement encouraged more than I can say, thank you Kelly, Mary, Stacey and Christine.

To the decade of students, now officers I've served at the United States Naval Academy (at our home by the bay), thank you for the honor of doing life with you. We've lived out the Word of God in our singing, dancing, laughing and traveling. We learned to represent Jesus to others and one another, and to work out every kink and challenge along the way – for all of it – I'm more grateful than I could ever express. He has done marvelous things! Fair winds and following seas, my loves.

Last and most importantly, I thank God whose hand was on this project before it even occurred to me. I thank you in advance for opening your hand and flinging *Steady Faith* wherever its message is needed in the earth. I am yours.

About the Author

In 2017, Karla released *Steady Faith: Navigate the detours, live your purpose, make a difference.* The book supports leaders, influencers and creatives in healthy examination of the state of their souls as they continue to lead others. She provides group and individual coaching, hosts workshops and webinars for leaders and is active as a speaker for corporations, universities and various groups.

Classical Singer

The versatile American soprano Karla Scott, possesses a voice of uncommon clarity and beauty of timbre, has been described by the Washington Post as "a vividly expressive soprano." Equally comfortable performing in various musical genres, Karla recently performed the soprano solo in Mozart's *Vesperae Solennes de Confessore* with the Maryland Summer Chorus and Orchestra under the direction of Dr. Cindy Bauchpies. In the spring of 2014, Karla performed the soprano solo in Verdi's *Requiem* with Annapolis Symphony and combined choruses of the United States Naval Academy.

Also in 2013, Karla along with collaborative pianist Alexei Ulitin premiered from *Slavery to Freedom*, a song cycle by American concert pianist and composer Alan Mandel at the University of Maryland, College Park. Mr. Mandel's settings of Henry Wadsworth Longfellow's *Poems on Slavery*, were juxtaposed with songs by Samuel Coleridge Taylor, the Anglo-African composer best known for his choral cantata, *Song of Hiawatha*. Scott has performed as soloist with the Samuel Coleridge-Taylor society based in Portland, Maine and was included in the documentary film featuring the composer's works.

Her work has included performances Mahler's *Resurrection Symphony* with Annapolis Symphony, the Villa-Lobos *Bachianas Brasileiras No. 5* (transcribed for 8 basses rather than 8 celli) and a filmed masterclass with famed mezzo-soprano Fredericka (Flicka) von Stade where Ms. Scott's performance drew rave reviews from von Stade.

In earlier seasons, Dr. Scott was soprano soloist for Mozart's *C Minor Mass,* in Annapolis; Maher Symphony No.4 in College Park, MD; Faure *Requiem* in College Park, MD; Serpina in Progress's *La Serva Padronna* in Greenville, NC; Clorinda in Rossini's *La Cenorentola* in Greenville, NC; Kathleen in Vaughn-Williams' *Riders to the Sea* in College Park, MD; Pamina in Mozart's *Die Zauberflote* in Rome, Italy. Ms. Scott sang special performances for the late Nelson Mandela, and for the funeral services of Rosa Parks. She has appeared at the Kennedy Center, the National Gallery of Art in Washington DC and in a film about the life of African-American composer, Jester Hairston

Choral Work

Dr. Scott's choirs have appeared at the 2014 Kennedy Center Honors in Washington, DC, on a goodwill tour of South Korea in 2011, at the 2008 Inauguration concert for President Barack Obama, in Zimbabwe, Africa with President Mugabe in attendance, and in Washington, D.C. for a United Negro College Fund celebration with former President Bill Clinton. In 2013 Karla partnered with Jazz at Lincoln Center to create a touring workshop introducing Mr. Marsalis' landmark work, "Abyssinian: A Gospel Celebration" to hundreds of secondary and college students in east coast and mid-western states. A tireless advocate for fostering connections between young people and the arts, Karla is an in-demand workshop and masterclass clinician.

Worship

As a worship leader and workshop presenter, Karla has served numerous churches and national and international conferences in the United States and Caribbean allowing her to fulfill the mandate on her life to make Jesus known through worship. She has shared ministry settings with many notable pastors, psalmists and recording artists in the body of Christ including Twinkie Clark, T.D. Jakes, Smokey Norful, Alvin Slaughter and had the opportunity to serve President Barack Obama and the first family as worship leader during MLK worship services in 2012. In 2017, Scott launched **The Power of Your Voice** interactive vocal coaching series that allows her to serve and support singers in the Body of Christ all over the world.

Academic

Ms. Scott has an earned *BM in Vocal Pedagogy* (the science of voice training) from East Carolina University, *MM in Vocal Performance* (opera concentration) from University of Maryland. In 2016 she earned a doctorate in music (vocal pedagogy concentration) from the University of Maryland, College Park. She has served as instructor of Music at Bennett College, adjunct faculty at the U.S. Naval Academy, and as adjunct faculty at the University of Maryland, College Park. Karla's doctoral dissertation research was interdisciplinary in nature and examined the intersection of gospel music, leadership development and American nationalism.

Connect with Karla
www.karlascott.net